It takes a little crazy to make a difference

(Dafna's Version)

ADVANCED PRAISE FOR IT TAKES A LITTLE CRAZY

"Coloradans have proven that finding the best solutions for the complex issues facing our state can be achieved by working together. Dafna Michaelson Jenet has taken that idea to all 50 states and has found Americans who are solving problems and building community"

- John W. Hickenlooper, US Senator and
former Governor, State of Colorado

"I could not believe what I was watching. A single mother quits her job, cashes in her 401k and launches off across the country to find people who want to make a difference. Period. Never mind that we are in the throes of a national economic meltdown. It is a cause. And people do for causes what they would never do for money. "I wanted to find the people who, when they see a problem, raise their hand and say, 'I'll take care of that,' says Dafna. The CBS Sunday Morning with Charles Osgood piece ended and I was speechless. Who is this woman? So I reached her via the internet and happily discovered that she was for real. And a little crazy. She found the stories she was looking for and when you read this book you will find your own story. And you too will get a little crazy—but you'll be smiling.

- Gary Dixon, President,
The Foundation for a Better Life

"There's a Chinese proverb which says, 'The journey is the reward.' Truer words could not be found to describe Dafna's amazing trips, the people she met and the stories she shares in this book. I was fascinated and inspired by Dafna at the beginning of her journey and am challenged by her to be a little crazy at its completion."

- Adam Schrager, Reporter/Author

"This book is inspiration with a bit of honey, a lot of humor and a full quart of hope. It's a road trip that plows neighborhoods for authentic leaders, grown local and building possibility. What we all want is here. The wish that change is possible and we can make it happen. Dafna Michaelson Jenet takes us across the country, state by state, and introduces us to regular folk who dramatically change community, one step at a time."

- Elaine Zimmerman
Executive Director, CT Commission on Children &
founder of Parent Leadership Training Institute

It takes a little crazy to make a difference

(Dafna's Version)

Dafna Michaelson Jenet

Storytellers Publishing
Colorado, USA

Storytellers Publishing
An imprint of Journey Institute Press,
a division of 50 in 52 Journey, Inc.
journeyinstitutepress.org

Library of Congress Control Number: 2024939933
Names: Michaelson Jenet, Dafna
Title: IT TAKES A LITTLE CRAZY TO MAKE A DIFFERENCE (DAFNA'S VERSION)
Description: Colorado: Storytellers Publishing, 2025

Identifiers: ISBN 979-8-9894379-9-3 (hardcover)
978-1-964754-02-4 (paperback)
978-1-964754-00-0 (ebook/kindle)
Subjects: BISAC:
BIOGRAPHY & AUTOBIOGRAPHY / Women
SOCIAL SCIENCE / Anthropology / Culture & Social
TRAVEL / United States / General

Second Edition
Printed in the United States of America

1 3 7 10 13 14 18 51 88 92

This book was typeset in Garamond / Anko

Cover Design by WiggleB Studios
Editing by: Jessica Medberry - InkWhale Editorial LLC

Contents

The moment I set eyes on him I knew.

He was different.

The tiny crinkles around his eyes as he smiled at me

told a story.

The moment his lips touched mine

a thousand lifetimes flashed before my eyes.

Kisses, centuries old,

filled with passion,

rose to the surface of my memory.

At last he found me.

At last we would be united once more.

At last our souls would form a solid bond and become one.

The moment I set eyes on him I knew.

The moment our lips met our promise was sealed.

For Michael,

my love.

Acknowledgements

I struggled with this acknowledgement page. As I discussed with my husband, the whole book is an acknowledgement. From the 500 incredible people I interviewed along this Journey to the thousands of others I met in each city, to those who read my blog and cheered me on and to those at home who held me up when I had so far left to go, I am grateful. You are the Journey.

To my children, you inspired me each day of my travels. There was not a minute that went by that you did not pop into my mind. Seeing the Journey through your eyes showed me quickly that I was foolish to believe that I could be your teacher. You are mine. I cherish you.

Michael. Without you this Journey would not have happened. More on that in the pages to come.

Foreword

Barry Petersen
CBS News Correspondent

"Not I, nor anyone else can travel that road for you.
You must travel it by yourself.
It is not far. It is within reach.
Perhaps you have been on it since you were born, and did not know.
Perhaps it is everywhere - on water and land."

- Walt Whitman, Leaves of Grass

There is a game I play looking out the window of the plane when I am landing in a new country, often sent there because a war is underway or maybe the country was targeted by nature's massive devastation. An earthquake. A tsunami.

I try to guess what is down there by looking at it from up here. What are they doing to one another, how are they surviving. Are they surviving? If it's a dangerous place, then there is one nagging question more: will I come home from this one.

That is how the journey begins. But once on the ground, once meeting and seeing people, and sometimes seeing their extraordinary resilience, it is no longer about seeing houses and streets and cars from a descending airplane. It is about faces and stories. So many stories. And my job is telling those stories on television. Dafna's was one such story.

What intrigued me about Dafna's plan to visit 50 states in 52 weeks, her "50 in 52", was its utter absurdity.

How can a divorced woman with children, on her own, with little money and no real resources, be crazy enough to want to visit 50 states and tell the lovely stories of people changing what they see around them?

We joined one of Dafna's visits when she went to Arizona and we also filmed people whose stories she had captured in Oklahoma, West Virginia, and San Francisco. This was for our story on *CBS Sunday Morning with Charles Osgood*. Being with her answered the questions. First, she never realized how absurd the whole project really was, so she just pushed forward. Second, she was fascinated by the people she met and what they were doing, and had an overwhelming curiosity to learn and tell their stories.

Finally, she has apparently never heard of the word "can't" because she just powered on, state by state, finding ordinary people who do extraordinary things. This book is about an amazing journey any one of us might have made...but she actually did.

And it is proof that life is not about journeys. Life is always about how journeys change you.

Introduction

You could have heard a pin drop. I stood there in the middle of the floor, my red suit feeling snug. My microphone's volume seemed too weak for the space it was supposed to fill. The silence in itself is not an unusual occurrence at a speaking engagement, but considering I was standing in the center of a gym with 1,500 middle school students, it was a bit unbelievable. My audience was packed into the bleachers, with overflow students sitting five deep on the hardwood floor of the basketball court. A young woman sitting on the floor had raised her hand. She appeared to be a seventh grader at most. Her face was round, and her waist-length blond hair was pulled back into a ponytail. I had pointed to call on her.

It is not often that I am caught off guard by an audience member's question, but this time I stopped and wondered if I'd heard her correctly.

"What does it feel like to change someone's life?"

Did she really ask me that? I never said I had changed someone's life. As a matter of fact, all I had done in the forty minutes preceding that question was share stories about others who were making an impact in the world. And yet, she wanted to know what it felt like to change someone's life. I guess I had never thought about it before. I have always wanted to make an impact on the world, but was I really changing people's lives? Had something I said changed hers?

Growing up was not easy for me. Is it for anyone? Is there anyone out there who can stand up and say, "My life, piece of cake?" We all have our burdens to carry. Mine was a burden of not fitting in. I always felt like I never fit anywhere. I didn't fit into my religious community. I didn't fit in at my school. I didn't fit nicely into a clique. I was often the "odd man out" in my youth group. I had friends, lots of them, but only a handful of people who completely "got" me—and even they would sometimes shake their heads in wonder at the schemes and plans and dreams I had.

When I did fit in, it was because I was working on something: an event, a meeting, an issue, a cause. I had passion and was driven to learn, and I always loved to travel. I thought of myself as a wanderer and a solo navigator. I followed the path that unfolded before me and took the challenges and opportunities one at a time.

And yet, I ached to fit in. I ached to belong to my religious community. I ached to be included in the parties my peers seemed to revel in. As I became an adult, I still found myself just one step outside anybody's inner circle. What was it about me that did not allow me to fit nicely into any box?

My entire life had been a journey, but where was the destination? When would I finally arrive? Could I really be someone who could change someone's life when my own was still in such flux?

Perhaps you picked up a copy of this book because you followed my 50 in 52 Journey. Perhaps you remember when I quit my job, during the worst economic cycle our country has faced in recent memory, to collect stories of ordinary people solving problems in their community. Perhaps you picked it up because you, too, secretly feel that you might be a little crazy, and you really want to make a difference in this world. Perhaps you are seeking answers or a roadmap. Whatever your reasons, I want to tell you a story—many of them, actually. I'll tell you about what I learned, and I'll even tell you about what I lost. Maybe within those stories you will see yourself reflected, and your own path or story will unwind. I hope you will share that story with me, and together we can embrace the journey of life in this world that we share.

When I speak to audiences about the 50 in 52 Journey, I start out by asking my listeners to jot down three things they've complained about in the last week. I ask them to think about those things that make repeat appearances in their daily gripe column. Now, I'm asking you. In the white space below, or on a fresh piece of paper, jot down three things that are on the top of your complaint list. Keep these complaints in mind as you read this book. As you get ideas for solving the challenges you've jotted down, make little notes for yourself in the margins.

Ready to jump in? I am! (I may have been born ready . . .) Let's go!

Chapter 1
The birth of a crazy idea

The year 2008 was a tumultuous time in America. Everyone felt it. The economy began to slip and then free fall. We were in the midst of the longest, most televised, and most in-your-face presidential campaign the country had seen. There was a war being battled a world away. At home, we were seemingly safe from the stray bullets, but our children were being sent into battle and were not coming back. It appeared that everything was out of our control, and I felt we were slipping into a deep well of depression. The image of America, "the land of opportunity," was being muddied, and we could not see past our own fears to figure out how to stop this free fall. I decided I could not sit idly by. I had to do something to stop it. I had to do it for me, for you, for my children. I had no master plan. I had not been dreaming up an action plan with vision, goals, and measurable outcomes. I did not have my sights set on creating a citizen stimulus plan. I didn't know *what*, I just knew *that* I had to do something.

Like many, I lay awake at night uncertain about the future, but what I was supposed to do was not crystallizing in my head. I had a mortgage. I had a job. My two children relied on me for security. Sure, they have their dad too, but he and I were no longer married, and it was up to me to make sure they had stability everywhere they lived. I had a new boyfriend and the future of that relationship looked promising, but no vows or long-term commitments had been exchanged. My life probably would have been OK if I had just kept going through the motions. While I loved the tasks involved, my job had reached a point where leaving was more enticing than staying, though the economy was working really hard to convince me otherwise. As I write this, I wonder if, at least for the short term, I'd have been better off not hitting the road . . .

Let me start by getting this off my chest: this was all Michael's fault. Michael, my new boyfriend, needed change. We had just finished our grocery shopping at Safeway and had already checked out. Michael looked toward the Customer Service counter and noticed that the lottery jackpot was up to $450,000,000. He casually suggested that to break the $20 we buy a lottery ticket. This was not a normal practice for him, but who was he to turn his nose up at a chance to win $450,000,000?

A childhood of weekly unanswered lottery prayers had destroyed any interest I had in this deceptive game. For all the love and all the powerful gifts my mother gave me growing up, the lottery ritual of "What will we do with the money we win?" broke my heart time and again. I knew the pull of the deceptively simple selection of the right six numbers that would change my life. We would no longer struggle. My stepfather would be able to quit his evening job. Each week, he worked evenings at the school bingo hall, exposing his lungs to the players' toxic cigarette smoke. He did this so my brothers and I could attend a private religious school. He gave us everything he had, as did my mother. Winning the lottery could have made their lives so much easier. Each week, the lottery failed my family. Each week, my disenchantment with the game grew.

I was paralyzed for a moment as I stood next to Michael at the Customer Service counter. I wanted to tell him about my sadness, my fear, and my raw anger at the lottery. What I did not want to do was reveal the full extent of my baggage right there in the middle of the grocery store. I did not want to risk turning him off, losing him. It's not so easy finding a boyfriend when you are a single mom with a mortgage and a tuition bill.

I gathered myself together. Instead of completely losing it, I simply said, "I don't play the lottery. But you can get a ticket and I'll pray for you to win."

Moments later, we were in the Safeway parking lot, walking hand in hand to the car. Michael, ever the gentleman, with his lottery ticket tucked safely away in his wallet, opened the door for me and helped me inside. He put the key in the ignition and looked over at me. As I visualize the moment in my mind, I am certain there was a mischievous glint in his eye. He then said the words that changed my life forever. "So, what are you going to do when we win the lottery?"

I was caught. I had to tell him why I wouldn't play. I couldn't handle going through the cycle of hope and loss. I told him my story. I hoped he'd let me off the hook. But ever the believer in positive energy and thinking, he said the only way to win was to play the game. So I played the game with my new love.

I'm only human. As much as I'd love to gloss over the things that, when I look back at them, show the chinks in the armor of the image I'd like to portray, I just can't. The first words out of my mouth when I agreed to play the game were not about the charities I'd support or the mountain of student loans I'd pay off. They were about my dream car, a black Porsche Cayenne with a custom leather interior. It would be the first hybrid off the line. I could see myself driving this ultimate sexy vehicle that would fly me to the mountains and swoop me through the city with elegance and grace. I could visualize heads turning as I got out of the Cayenne, as people wondered who could be driving such a spectacular car. There was no way I'd admit it to Michael, but I was having fun playing the game.

Then he asked, "Will you travel?" Once again, the world stood still for just a moment. My life would forever be altered by my reply.

My mind did not miss a beat. "Of course I'll travel. As a matter of fact, I'm going to visit all fifty states and I'm going to meet with every governor. I'm going to ask them how they are engaging their citizens in solving community problems." Just like that, out the words flew. I did not know where they had come from.

The look on Michael's face showed he expected a more normal answer, something like, "Yeah, I'd go to Fiji." Once the floodgates opened, I was making plans. I was certain the governors would meet with me; after all, I had lottery winnings to contribute freely to their campaigns. We talked for hours about the trip: the logistics, the conversations, the importance it would have to the people of America. I would single-handedly fight to strengthen America and to ensure that their individual voices and ideas were heard.

As I drifted off to sleep early that night, my mind was filled with the dream. I imagined that maybe the travels of a single mom, seeking and sharing the stories of ordinary citizens who were engaging in the process of making our country better, might give others the encouragement they needed—encouragement to jump into the game and take control of what was bringing them and their communities down. Before I took my last conscious breath, I could taste it. We had to win that lottery.

With the first morning light, I reached over to my nightstand and grabbed my BlackBerry. I shot off a text to Michael, asking him to tell me we had won the lottery.

He could not oblige.

For a moment, I felt that familiar shattering of my prayers.

In the next moment, I decided I had to take this journey with or without money from the lottery.

This was Michael's chance to discourage me, to give me the line I'd heard so often in my life: "You can do that when we have more money." But he didn't. In fact, he did the exact opposite. He encouraged me. Before I left for the office, I had emailed several people whom I considered to be my mentors, arranging coffee and lunch meetings for the following day. As I laid out the plan, I could see my listeners' eyes grow wide. Without hesitation, many of them told me I was a nut, crazy, off my rocker. They told me it was impossible, and in the same breath, they encouraged me, saying that if anyone could pull it off, I could. They believed, as I did, that people would become inspired. Simply by hearing about the concept, my listeners already were. This feedback drove me, and before I knew it, we had a board of directors who met at my house to discuss the logistics.

The board consisted of a political reporter, a lawyer, a law student, a nonprofit professional, a lobbyist, a successful businessman, and Michael. We were crowded into my small living room, which I had cleverly sectioned into a dining room and sitting area, while my two young children slept soundly upstairs. Most of the board members were gathered around the table, and I was sitting on my couch. I answered the questions they fired at me, and we attempted to hammer out a mission statement to prepare for a press release that would allow us to begin the task of raising money for the Journey.

In a moment of inspiration, as we were discussing the logistics of reaching out to and capturing the attention of the governors, the political reporter jumped out of his chair and asked, "What do you need the governors for? What you are talking about here are the ordinary citizens doing extraordinary things for their communities. Don't you want to find the people who self-select? Those who do not wait to be asked?"

This is one of those moments where I'd love to leave out what was actually going through my head, but I won't. I owe it to you to share, because in that instant, that comment may have altered the course of my life and made the Journey what it was.

For everyone else in the room, it was crystal clear. He was absolutely right. The governors were not the focus of this exercise. The governors were not going to inspire a nation. The governors were not likely to give me the time of day. But I wanted to meet the governors. At that moment, if you had asked me what I wanted to be when I grew up, I would have told you that my goal was to one day become governor of the state of Colorado. I wanted to meet the governors, both to find out how they worked (as research for my own future) and to encourage them to reach out to their citizens. I knew, beyond a shadow of a doubt, that the members of the communities they led knew how to strengthen their states and shape their neighborhoods. The governors, I felt, simply needed to do a better job of engaging people in the process.

I sat there quietly, squeezed as far as I could push my body into the corner of the couch, snuggling a throw pillow in front of me. I was reconciling the direction my Journey had just taken and fighting what felt like the selfish desire to stick to my guns on the governor thing. All while realizing that the reporter's epiphany truly would make the Journey a journey for America.

Before the crew left my house, we had hammered out a press release, begun the process for filing a 501c3 nonprofit business classification, talked through the timing for leaving my job, and created the Journey's tagline: "One single mom, fifty states, fifty-two weeks, a Journey to find the people moving America forward." We had already secured the URL www.50in52journey.com.

The next morning, I dropped my kids off at school early and rushed to Michael's house. I needed to speak with him. When I got there, he was in the bathroom shaving. I looked at this man and saw the softness in his eyes and the love in the tiniest crease lines around them. I wanted to stroke his unshaven face. I stood behind him, talking into the mirror as he continued his morning ritual. I felt the way a little girl must feel watching her daddy. I never did that with my own father.

My relationship with this man was so different from anything I had ever experienced. He was six foot one, with broad shoulders, blond hair, and twinkling green-brown eyes that devoured me with their intense love, and I was entirely smitten with him. I caught his eyes watching me. He stopped and looked at me quizzically. I was so nervous, and I had to get this out on the table. I asked if he understood he was going to be the one to lose out on this deal.

We had figured out the night before that if I traveled only on the days my children were with their father, we could make this work logistically. I could be on the road Wednesday through Friday most weeks, and every other weekend. When I was home, I'd be dedicating my time to being Mommy. I was excited because this also meant that, for the first time in my children's lives, I'd be available during normal working hours to take part in things like Girl Scouts with my daughter and Tae Kwon Do with my son. My boyfriend would be losing out. Until this point in our relationship, the time I was not with my children was focused on him, and all of that was about to change.

He put down his razor and turned to look me in the eyes as he held my face in his large, soft hands. He said, "This is too important not to do." He kissed me gently on my lips and went about continuing his preparations. I stood glued to the floor, having never felt so supported or loved in my life. I knew at that moment that I had won the lottery.

Chapter 2
Finding courage

Three weeks before I was supposed to leave for my first state, I had not even purchased the first airplane ticket for the fifty-state Journey I was supposed to embark upon. I had been completely paralyzed by fear. The week I left my job was the exact week the banks began their historic collapse. My peers, who, just days before, were gung ho about my crazy endeavor, were now looking at me skeptically and wondering aloud if I should ask for my job back. I headed off to Israel on a trip I had won, and when I returned to America three weeks later, the country was in an all-out financial panic.

Funders who were planning to hold events for me backed out. Close mentors and advisors told me I could not do it. One woman looked me straight in the eyes and said, "Get on your hands and knees and crawl back to the hospital and beg for your job back."

I was caught. I had been talking to everyone I could for close to seven months about this Journey. I was doing it because Americans were spiraling down into an abyss of depression and feeling a total lack of control. I was certain I could make a difference by changing the way we looked at ourselves. I was going to be the mirror that reflected who we truly are as a society. That mirror would encourage people to take control and take action. If we needed reassurance that we had a strong community before the collapse, how much more so did we need it after?

There was no way I could even begin to think of backing down. I had made a commitment. There was also no way I could think of to fund it.

I don't come from money. I did not have access to any great pocket of wealth. The long process of obtaining IRS approval for our 501c3 application precluded me from receiving grant monies, the availability of which was disappearing before our eyes anyway.

It was the holiday season, and each party I attended was subdued. While my former assistant, Amanda, and I drove to the Colorado Healthcare Directors of Volunteer Service party, we made idle chat. I asked about her daughter Erika, and Amanda beamed with pride as she told me about her daughter's new beauty business, which Erika had funded partly with a loan from her 401(k).

I heard nothing else Amanda said for the remaining hour of our drive. All I kept thinking was "I have a 401(k)." I had found my money. I rationalized that at thirty-six, I had time to rebuild my retirement savings. And even if it meant working for the rest of my life, the contribution to America and the experience of truly learning about my country's people were worth it. It was three weeks before I was supposed to leave for Delaware.

The money problem "figured out," I had at least enough to get started; I just had to get moving on the rest of the arrangements. Those who knew I was still going to do this Journey kept asking how excited I was. They glowed when we talked about my upcoming adventure. I assured them I was quite excited, while inside I was filled with panic.

I lay awake each night wondering what I had done. How was I going to pull this off? When my mother would voice her concern and my grandmother would emphasize her worry on the phone to me, I assured them it would be fine. Meanwhile, my brain was screaming, "Are you completely out of your mind?"

Leaving for Delaware was a surreal experience. I was panicked. The board and I had selected Delaware as my first state to visit. It felt appropriate to kick off the Journey there, in the first state in the Union. I did not have a single interview scheduled. The economy had collapsed beneath us. I wasn't sure I'd be able to figure out the camera, mic, and tripod. What the heck was I doing?

Michael drove me to the airport and took my suitcase from the back of the car. I could see the panic in my eyes reflected in his. "If all else fails," he said, "just go to a coffee shop and talk to people." Michael is always fond of saying that I could talk to a telephone pole and have an interesting conversation. I was not so sure.

The truth of the matter is that while on the outside I look like a classic extrovert, on the inside I'm more of an introvert. I get nervous walking into parties or social situations where I don't know anyone—and even when I do know the people. It is something I've been working on my whole life. When it boils down to it, I'm actually shy, and I'm most comfortable at home or in intimate settings. I recharge my batteries in those silent, solitary moments. How on earth was I going to muster the courage to do this?

I knew that if I was going to pull this off at all, I needed to start actually getting excited. Exactly two weeks before I was to head out to Delaware, while snuggled up in my bed after another restless night, I decided that today was the day to get excited. I talked to myself about the amazing adventure that lay in front of me. I talked to myself about the people I was going to meet. I talked to myself about the impact these people would have on the rest of the country. The same things I said to everyone I met when sharing about the Journey, I told myself. I started to feel excited.

I forced a huge, painful smile, hoping to trick the endorphins in my brain into kicking into full gear. My mood lifted, and I got out of bed feeling pumped and ready to rock the world. As I began to brush my teeth, my smile still forced to maximum intensity, I gagged and began to vomit blood. Dark red blood started streaming out of my nose while seeming to pour from my mouth. My bathroom sink and mirror were covered, and I could hear my children stirring in the other room.

I used my foot to close the bathroom door so the kids would not see the bloody mess. I just kept thinking, "I'm not supposed to die now! I'm just beginning my Journey." Indeed, I knew I was just beginning my life. I pulled myself together. I managed to stop the nosebleed and cleaned up the bathroom. I dropped the kids off at school and then had to figure out what was wrong with me.

I had already lost my insurance, so I could not go to the doctor. I called a physician friend. He assured me it was likely I had simply developed a nosebleed while sleeping, and the blood had pooled in my stomach, causing the vomiting . . . I wasn't going to die.

I knew I should be relieved, but now I was really scared. With dying off the table, I had no more excuses. I sucked it up, bought my plane ticket to Delaware, and began a veritable storm of emails and phone calls. I was desperately trying to find people in Delaware who were "helping to solve community problems or otherwise working to build community," as I was posting on social media for every statewide search. I even stopped a car at the busy intersection of 17th and Colorado Boulevard that had Delaware license plates. Jumping out of my car, engine still running, I began tapping on their window in the rain. As the young female passenger timidly cracked the window a bit, I slid my business card in and asked her if she knew of anyone who fit the bill.

On January 7, 2009, armed with my BlackBerry, my laptop, my cameras and tripod, and a few items of clothing, I boarded the flight to Delaware. I knew that there were two possible outcomes: colossal failure or astronomic success. I was not about to come home admitting defeat.

"What are you looking for? Can you be more specific?" That was the most common response when I sent out requests seeking "the people who are solving community problems or otherwise working to build community." It was too vague, I was told. People needed me to tie it in a neater bow. Are you looking for people working on homelessness? Education? The environment? I would always respond by asking, "Are those the problems affecting your community?"

I wasn't trying to be flippant, but I also did not want this to be a Journey of "my" issues. I really wanted to understand what was going on and what was moving America. All the way to Delaware, I grappled with this. Perhaps I would have had more scheduled interviews if I had specifically selected the issues I wanted to discuss and the people I wanted to meet.

As soon as the plane's wheels screeched to a stop at Philadelphia International Airport, I turned on my BlackBerry. It began to buzz incessantly as it ticked off the emails and voicemails I had received while disconnected from technology on the four-hour flight. I scrolled through my email and was filled with both relief and a new sense of nervousness and urgency. All of a sudden, I had a full roster of interviews ahead of me.

I headed out of the airport and toward the rental car lot, nervous energy coursing through my body. I approached the counter and suddenly realized I was not sure what to do. It hadn't occurred to me until then that this would be my first time renting a car on my own. I got married at twenty-two, before I was old enough to rent a car. And, since I had been in that marriage for close to twelve years, whenever a car needed to be rented, my husband took care of it. I sat in the driver's seat and figured out where everything was. A feeling of liberation washed over me. As I basked in my glow, I was smacked back to reality when I realized I couldn't figure out how to start the car.

Chapter 3
Who am I?

I was born in Israel in 1972. My parents had such a romantic tale. A young American following her roots, my mother was a beautiful girl with long, flowing brown hair, thin as thin could be, with a spirit that was at times tortured and at times inspired. She had left the US behind and was determined to make new roots in the land of her ancestors.

My father was a young sailor in the US Navy. His mother was an ardent Zionist, and moving to Israel was my father's way of living out his mother's dreams. My parents met at the Immigration Absorption Center, and their passion turned to love, marriage, and me.

Life was very hard in Israel in 1972. My father missed his family desperately. He decided to move the family back to the United States. My mother never forgave him.

They thought life was hard in Israel, but I will tell you that for me, life was hard in the US. I remember the electricity being cut off when we did not have enough money to pay the bill. Two more children and a divorce later, my family was struggling. I remember standing in line for food stamps and my mother making the agonizing choices between orange juice, shoes, and milk. Which did we truly need? We could not afford all three.

I only knew we were poor because my mother sent us to a Jewish private school. The one around the corner from us would not give us a scholarship, so she put us on a bus and we traveled a fair distance to get to the one that would. I did not have what the other kids had, and that was how I knew we were poor.

The apartment complex where we lived, now a gentrified part of Queens, was a glorified project. While living there, I watched a man get stabbed. I watched the playground set aflame by a group of teenagers. I watched a little boy blow his eye out with a firecracker that had not gone off as expected. And one day, I followed a woman to her apartment where she molested me, something I have never spoken of before.

I spent every single night in my bed in fear. I was afraid of the cockroaches and mice in my apartment. I was afraid of the cat we had gotten to take care of the rodents. I was afraid of the noises outside my window. I was afraid that someone would enter in the middle of the night and kidnap me. I would lie absolutely still, not wanting to move a muscle, until my mother would come into the room and tell us to get ready for school. I feared that an intruder who found me awake would have to kill me.

When my mother remarried, stability began to enter my world. My family was still poor for a long time, but we were climbing out of it. Every day brought us one step closer to a middle-class existence. When my abba, the Hebrew word for father and the name I call my stepfather (as I do not believe that "step" applies), got a job in Cincinnati, Ohio, I was sure that we had won the lottery. I thought we somehow went from poor to rich in one fell swoop.

While I learned quickly that, economically, we were still at the bottom of the neighborhood food chain, it did not matter. For the first time in my life, I felt safe. I was eleven years old.

At fourteen, I started formulating my own ideas and opinions. I would sit around on Sabbath afternoons and listen to my parents and their lunch guests talk about all the things that were wrong in the community, or the neighborhood, or the city, or the world. They would discuss solutions that I thought were brilliant! As the weekend melted into the week, I would observe with frustration that no one took any action on those brilliant solutions. I simply did not understand this. So, at fourteen years of age, I promised solemnly to never complain about a problem unless I was willing to work on the solution. This became a guiding, and sometimes driving, principle in my life, which to this day inspires so many of the decisions I make.

At fourteen years old, what this principle meant for me was making choices to volunteer and to join a youth group that reflected my beliefs and values. It also meant making some very tough religious decisions.

I was raised in a traditional Orthodox Jewish home. We kept strictly kosher and observed the Sabbath to the letter of the law. Those two items in and of themselves were not challenges for me. However, many other laws presented insurmountable challenges every day, especially those that regulated modesty in dress and prevented me from singing in public, a passion and dream. I did not fit in at the Jewish day school I attended. I did not fit in at the Jewish youth group connected with my synagogue.

I begged my mother to let me attend public school, and then begged even more for permission to attend the Cincinnati School for the Creative and Performing Arts (SCPA). She allowed it and fully honored my needs, which gave her a bad name and reputation in the community, and cemented my place as the black sheep in my family.

With each step forward, I tried to figure out who I was in this world. I became very active in a Jewish (though non-denominational) youth group and started taking educational and leadership roles. I traveled to Poland at seventeen to visit the Nazi concentration camps, and I became even more acutely aware of who I was as a whole being. As I grew and became more connected to my Judaism, I thought I'd give Orthodoxy another attempt. Instead of attending the College-Conservatory of Music as I had planned, I chose to attend Stern College for Women—an Orthodox Jewish college in New York.

From there, I closely (at least, closely for me) followed the path I thought I was supposed to. I married right out of college and became immersed in my Orthodox community. My new husband and I started a fresh life together in Colorado. Kids followed, and then the marriage failed. All the while, I was still trying to jam my square self into the round hole of Orthodoxy.

By the end of my marriage, I had given up the battle. I knew that so much was awry when I compared the way I felt at home to the way I felt in synagogue. I needed a clean break.

My professional life had been the crowning glory for me. I enjoyed my work. I had good jobs. I followed paths, almost never applying for a job without first knowing they wanted me for it. I volunteered in the community. I went to graduate school. I was growing and forming and learning about myself and realizing, step by step, that the headache I felt was from that incessant hammer trying to get me into that hole. It wasn't going to happen, and I had to make a change.

Leaving my marriage was the hardest decision I ever had to make. And because I loved my husband so much, I tried to come back and ended up having to leave it all over again. We did not work. We had very different goals and dreams and understandings of the world. I needed to find the right partner so I could be whole for myself, for my children, and for whomever that partner would be.

I met Michael during the initial breakup with my husband. We remained friends while I reunited with my husband and ultimately finalized the divorce. I was frightened of the chemistry I felt when I was around him. I liked him a lot, and we shared many of the same interests and passions. And I was physically attracted to him—very, very attracted to him. But he was not Jewish, and loving him would mean losing my family. I was raised knowing that if I married outside of the faith, I would be as if dead to the family. As much as I wanted Michael, I did not want to lose my family.

About three months after my divorce was final, the heat went out in my condo. I called Michael to come fix it . . . and, well, that was that. I knew somehow, some way, I needed to be together with him for the rest of eternity. I just didn't know how I was going to make that happen and not lose everything that was left of my bonds with my family.

Why am I telling you this story?

It is important to me that you know a few things about me before I relive this Journey with you.

1. I love my family profoundly. I love the way they live their lives. I love my siblings, all 7 of them, their spouses, and their children. I respect them deeply. I often look at their lives and try to imagine what mine might have been like if I had been happy in the trappings of a traditional Orthodox Jewish existence. Sometimes it feels so neat and easy. Then I remember my areas of angst and dissonance, which are still very real for me.

2. My children are everything to me. During the 50 in 52 Journey, many nameless people on blogs criticized me for traveling to the extent that I did during that year. To them, it must have meant I neglected my children's needs in some way. But it was during this year that both my children told me I was their hero. I firmly believe that if we want our children to grow up and be their fullest and most positive selves, then we must model that in whatever way makes sense for us.

3. I know how lucky I am to have found the friend, partner, and lover I have in Michael. Nothing else, just thought you should know.

Chapter 4
The harsh reality

You also need to know what I lost throughout this Journey. I am a positive person by nature. I truly have always tried to find the silver linings, and when I can no longer find them, I know I need to make changes. It is hard for me to talk about what I lost during this Journey, for so many reasons. I will open myself up to criticism, and I suppose that's OK. Perhaps I've lost that need for approval? No, but maybe I am OK if not everyone agrees with all the choices I have made. I lost a lot.

I lost my income.

Yes, I quit my job knowing full well what was going on in the economy. I also believed I'd be able to fundraise and cobble together enough, between that and my savings, to keep up with my lifestyle. I was wrong. Along with my income, I lost my insurance, and then got sick. By the middle of the Journey, I could no longer feed myself. Although I relied heavily on Michael for food and for my kids' needs, I ultimately ended up on food assistance and Medicaid. I never told anybody about this. It felt like I was keeping a dirty secret of failure. I cannot begin to tell you the extent of my embarrassment and shame as I sat in the waiting room at the Department of Human Services for my first appointment. People I knew, who were in the leadership there, walked by. I attempted to make myself invisible so as not to be found out. Dignity, I lost that too.

While the people I met along this Journey all took their own unique paths to creating lasting change in their lives and the lives of those around them, not all left jobs and security behind, but some did.

What was it that made some take that giant leap? The first story that comes to mind is that of Chris Grundner. A young man in his thirties, clean cut with brown hair and eyes and a corporate look, he was my second interview of the Journey. He had lost his best friend, his young wife Kelly, to brain cancer. They had been in Delaware, living out their dreams. They had good jobs and a good life when all of a sudden, Kelly fell ill. Warning signs were missed. By the time they went for help, it was too late. Kelly was only thirty-one when she died.

Dafna with Chris Grundner

Chris was devastated. He had sat by her side every moment until she passed. After Kelly was gone, Chris told his family and friends that he was going to leave his job and start the Kelly Heinz-Grundner Brain Tumor Foundation. He wanted to make sure no one else would miss the warning signs. Chris was determined to help those who were struggling through the disease process, as he and Kelly had.

Chris's friends thought he was simply in a grief spiral. His family begged him not to leave his job. He was on track to reach even higher levels of corporate success. But Chris knew what he had to do, and this was it.

After that interview, I often thought about Chris's single-minded focus. He clearly saw the path in front of him. He had a vision of how to do it. He made it a success. Chris was able to withstand the constant barrage of doubts and questions from family and friends as he carried out his mission.

As I continued with the Journey, I was less certain. My plan didn't feel focused to me. I was not working on one issue. Even as I looked at Chris's success, I was not certain I could replicate it. I don't fit into a nice office with a tight mission and single-minded focus on a cause. There was that hammer over my head once more, trying to pound me into a round hole. I don't have the round gene. I am edgy. I once dreamed that I was in a box trying to figure out how to get out. I saw a bright light shining from one of the corners, and I approached it. I climbed out of the box and leaped into uncertainty. I can clearly recall the sensation of falling as I passed through groups of people, all clamoring to pull me back. I follow paths, blazing new trails along the way, but at the core, I may always be the square peg.

I lost my house.

Yes, it was 2009 and many lost their homes, but I struggled with my choices, knowing full well they impacted this loss. I was embarrassed. I relived the fear from my childhood. Each night, I lay awake wondering if tonight was the night the police would come and escort me out of my home. With help from friends, I put the house on the market as a short sale. I never did get "sheriffed out," as my grandmother and her siblings did during the Depression, but I feared it every night.

In Indianapolis I met Andrea De Mink. Andrea was an average-height, feisty woman with wild blond hair and an unstoppable smile. One day, as she stepped out of her office on her lunch break, she saw a man digging through the trash to find his lunch. As she went to have her own lunch, she could not get the image of the man out of her head.

The next day, Andrea bought a huge bag of freezer pops. She sat in the middle of Monument Circle, a solitary woman with a bag of popsicles. She handed a popsicle out to whoever came toward her, mostly homeless men. Andrea tried to speak with them. She wanted to know their stories.

It would take a few more efforts, as popsicles turned to bottled water and sandwiches, before the men began to trust her. Andrea started asking them about their lives. She wanted to know about their hopes and their dreams. She wanted to figure out what made someone homeless and what kept them there.

Andrea was not homeless. She had some stability in her life. She put herself out there on the street day after day, until she began organizing and ultimately opened the PourHouse, an organization to address homelessness. Andrea had nailed it down. She figured out that she must reconnect homeless people in her community with their dreams. "One size does not fit all," Andrea is fond of saying when it comes to programs to end chronic homelessness. This "size"—this reconnection to dreams—was one step in the process for Andrea.

I was not homeless. Yes, I lost my home, with both hands on the reins of my dreams. They may have slipped for a while, but they are firmly gripped once more. As I move forward from this part of my story, I am reminded of a young woman in New York, Julie Gilbert, who dedicated a year of her life to serving in a soup kitchen. When I asked her what she had learned so far, she said, "We are only one flip of a coin away from being on the other side of the line."

I lost friends.

There were people in my life that could not understand what I was doing and why, and they simply felt they could no longer be my friends. At first, I was so distressed by this and by the other friends who never seemed to "get" what I was doing. Upon reflection, I realized it was OK that they didn't get it, or get me. This Journey was a big leap for many people. It was for me. Those who were true friends stayed with me. Some friends had to leave for a while and came back when they were ready. Those who did not come back were never truly friends to begin with. Taking a crazy Journey is almost as good as getting divorced for figuring out who is really on your team.

I began identifying certain shared experiences that the people I was meeting went through as they strengthened their communities. One of the strongest of these experiences was solitude. Many times, Andrea De Mink felt very alone in her struggle to create futures for the homeless people of Indianapolis. Her family and friends did not understand her. Time and again, I learned from the misunderstood people fighting for their communities.

I learned from Karl Hammer, in Vermont. He had to fight his neighbors, who claimed he was violating the law by farming (the country's cleanest and most odor-free) compost on his land. I learned from Eve Lapin, in Texas. She fought for doctors to spend time and resources to find a way to stop ALD, the genetic disease that killed her son and struck her nephews as well.

And, I learned from Embra Jackson, a middle-aged black man with a receding hairline and an easy smile, in Jackson, Mississippi.

He lost his friends and colleagues when he left the business world to join the Methodist ministry. It may take the people around you a little while—sometimes a long while—to catch up with you and understand what you are doing.

Embra recalled his friends saying, "I just don't know who you are anymore," and removing him from their Christmas card lists. Only once he completed his studies, joined the ranks of the ministry, and began impacting people's lives did his friends begin to return. As they saw the fruits of Embra's labors, they found their way back to him and came to respect his decisions. It was a very lonely process for Embra, but he stuck to his guns. He knew that what he was doing would add value to the community and the world.

I experienced this isolation, this loss of friends. Some of the people who advised me before the Journey and then changed their tunes as the economy collapsed became distant when I decided to forge ahead with my plans. I could not turn my back on the Journey I had planned. Whether I had the money or not, whether I had the support of my friends or not, I had made a commitment. I had identified a problem, and I could not, I would not, turn my back on the country now.

For months before the major banks collapsed, I had been telling people that I knew the answer. I had to show people the amount of good being accomplished in this country. I had to show people the other side of the news. I had to share authentic stories of everyday people taking charge and solving problems. If I did that, I knew we could learn how to change the mirror we used to reflect who we are as a society. Americans would see that there is real hope for our future. People would see that possibility lay within each of us.

How could I not act? Stepping back from my big idea would make me no different from all the adults who, I had felt, let me down in my childhood by their inaction. I had told my children what I was going to do. How could I let them down? I knew in my gut that what I was going to do would make a difference. How could I let myself down?

Many people did not understand my choice. Many of my close friends questioned me over and over again. They questioned my sensibilities. They questioned my dedication to my children. They questioned my love for Michael. They called me selfish. My parents were panicked. I sent my grandmother into a year of devout nightly prayer. She prayed for my safety and my health.

Again, I lost friends. And people I thought were friends. Some came back after the Journey, some did not. But I made many hundreds of new friends on my Journey—soulmates, to be exact. To be sure, there were many days of isolation along the way.

With that out of the way, I am sharing this story because I hope there is something you can take away. I hope you will take away the knowledge that if you want to do something crazy, something you believe will make an impact on your life, that you can, and that many others have come before you and done just that.

I want you to know that you don't need to ask permission, and you don't need to wait to be asked. You know what is bothering you. You feel it every day. You have the power inside of you to change that which no longer serves you. You may not want to do it alone, so find a partner or cheerleader. Yes, you may lose some friends along the way. The real ones, those who truly have your best interests at heart—they'll come back, you'll see. And, if you can't find a cheerleader, call me. I'll cheer you on during your journey.

I also want you to know that we are all wounded in our own ways. I have not shared all my wounds and all the chinks in my armor, but I have them. You have them. Not one of us gets through this life unscathed, but that does not make you less than anyone else. Own your power. It belongs to you alone. No one has the right to take that away. Indeed, no one has the ability; only you can let someone have your power. I implore you to keep it and use it to better your world and the world of those around you. No one else needs your power more than you.

During the 50 in 52 Journey, Michael bought me a bracelet in the Las Vegas airport that said "Embrace the Journey." That bracelet appeared

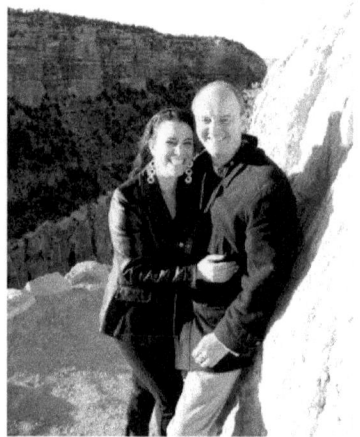

Dafna and Michael - Nevada

at a time when I was riddled with fear. I just had no idea how I was going to get this Journey done, and I was certain that I'd simply made a colossal mess of my life. I put the bracelet on, and as I drove through state after state, I would repeat out loud, "Embrace the journey, embrace the journey," on and on until I did. It was a rough road. I almost quit . . .

Embrace the journey.

Chapter 5
What did I find?

Before I started the Journey, I was telling everyone I met that I was going to find the ordinary people solving problems in their community. I was going to become the mirror that reflected who we truly are as a society. I'd share stories of good people. People who were working every day to make life a little better for themselves and their families. I know our world is mostly made up of really good people, even if the news focuses so much on those who slip up, who make mistakes, who suffer from mental illness without the support they need. I knew intrinsically that the evening news did not reflect the true nature of our society, yet there was no place to see what that honest reflection looked like.

And, yes, I found all of that and so much more.

I found people—five hundred of them, to be exact. People aged fourteen to ninety-one, from a plethora of religions and races and socioeconomic backgrounds, from the recently homeless to multibillionaires and everything in between. People who stood up and said, "I have a problem and you might have that problem too, and I'm going to solve it for both of us." They were not geniuses. Well, maybe some were. Mostly, they were ordinary people. Many of them had the same amount of money or education as you may have. They were people who were pushed—by necessity, their children, an internal drive, or G-d*—to solve a problem. (*Please note: throughout the book, I use the G-d spelling in the way I was taught to be most respectful. The complete spelling, with an "o" in place of the dash, is reserved for holy documents.)

I did not uncover any secret magic pill. These people used what little they had (or didn't have). They made it up. They tried and failed and tried again. I found real people, solving real problems, just as I had anticipated.

When we hear the term "real people," we may think "ordinary people." I found ordinary people. But what if ordinary is the new extraordinary, or vice versa—what if extraordinary is the new ordinary?

I am ordinary. My mother and stepfather raised me and my two brothers in a middle-class suburb of Cincinnati, Ohio, starting from just before my twelfth birthday. We struggled financially to keep up with the neighbors, though not nearly as much as my family did during my first decade of life. My parents scraped and scrimped to send us to a local private school, and I rebelled, begging to be sent to public school. I married a man I first dated at age sixteen, and we went off to forge our own life after finishing college. We had two kids; we grew and learned about ourselves and divorced. Ordinary.

What if inside everybody's "ordinary," there were particles that once fused to create the brilliance we see as extraordinary? I see no magical explanation in what created my passions. Yes, my family struggled with poverty in my early years. Yes, I was worried about food and safety. Yes, I remember my parent's divorce and the shift away from what, as a very young girl, I was certain was the nucleus of security. But how does that make me any different from you or anybody else? The challenges and pains of growing up are certainly unique for each of us. Ordinary is unique for each of us. Extraordinary is in each of us, and I can prove it.

My moment of extraordinary came during a dark phase of my life that was just beginning to lighten. I had been divorced just shy of a year. For the first time in my life, I lived alone. Well, technically not alone—there were my two children, ages seven and five, who were struggling with the divorce and continually asking me, "Why?" The nights they stayed with their father, per the terms of our shared custody agreement, were torturous for me. I missed them. I cried at night. Certainly there was a freedom that came with "nights off," but with my covers pulled up, my house too quiet, and no one I could kiss and sing prayers to at night, I felt lost. I was working my way through my new reality—and working on getting dates, a herculean task for a single mom. It was 2008 in ordinary America, and our lives were about to take a drastic turn.

I was seeking to share ordinary people's inspiring stories, and I found those stories. I found they came from humans in every size, shape, color, creed, faith, and age. To build community was simply to understand that your life is greater than those living with you in your four walls.

I learned that it was crucial to remember the roots of the people who built the America we see today. I add these next words carefully, as I learned the history of this country from the people native to this land during the Journey, and I understand how their communities suffered due to the settlers' ignorance and fear. So I say this with deference to our Native American hosts: when the pioneers began creating futures for their families in America, they understood that in order to succeed, they not only had to plant their fields and build their barns—they also had to help their neighbors plant *their* fields and build *their* barns. And when they were done with that, they came together to build first a church and then a schoolhouse. They did it together, not because someone offered them a grant to collaborate, as has become so popular in philanthropy today, but because they understood, fundamentally, that they were all in this together. If they succeeded, they succeeded as a community. If they failed, they failed as a community. They were far from home, and community was the only answer.

Today, it is no different. The people I met not only solved the problems facing their families, their children, or their businesses; the programs and projects they started helped many people around them as well.

People like Vicki and Stu LaRoche of Suwanee, Georgia. Vicki and Stu are a handsome American couple. Vicki, a short woman with cropped brown hair and a face that shows love, concern, and determination, and Stu, a tall, thin man with neatly cut brown hair, were raising three beautiful children. Vicki was mostly at home, and doing volunteer work in her church. Stu worked for UPS. When their eldest daughter stopped progressing mentally and emotionally around the age of twelve, they saw a series of doctors, who put her through a battery of tests to see what had suddenly stunted her advancement. Many, many months passed, and no doctor had the answer. One doctor told them, "Love your daughter as she is, her cognitive development is done."

Their daughter's body continued to develop into the body of a woman, but her mind had stopped—a rare and very late-presenting developmental disability. At around the same age, their youngest son also stopped developing.

Vicki threw herself into figuring out the systems of care and activities available to her children. However, she soon learned that at age twenty-two, it was all over. Their daughter's life became a broken record: bagging groceries for a few hours and spending the rest of her waking hours on the couch in front of the TV. Naturally, she became very isolated and depressed.

Knowing that the same future awaited her baby boy, who was now a young man, Vicki, her husband, and their middle son pondered what to do. It was actually the middle son who encouraged Vicki to start a nonprofit to create programs for people who, like their daughter, were stuck in isolation. Vicki was scared, but right about that time, UPS offered early retirement to Stu. He took it, and together the LaRoches created The Next Stop.

The Next Stop, in the model of the pioneers, helped not only the LaRoches but also dozens of families in the Suwanee area. The "kids" get together several times a week to play volleyball, cook creative treats, and go on outings. They have an opportunity to socialize and interact with people their own age, whose emotional development and communication abilities differ from the mainstream. The lives of the "kids" and their families have vastly improved because the LaRoches understood they were not in this alone.

Dafna with the LaRoches

There was nothing out of the ordinary about Vicki and Stu. They are your average everyday Americans, trying to get by and give their children the best shot at a good future. They figured out how to run an organization. They figured out how to spread the word. They figured out they could do it, simply because they cared enough to make it happen.

I point out Vicki and Stu because they are just like the many hundreds of people I interviewed around our glorious country. They are just like you, and just like me. They were going through life, and because they recognized the problem, they filled the need. Nobody asked them to do it. If they had not done it, who knows if another would have stepped up in their place.

Their magic was the encouragement of an energetic son, and their love for all three of their children.

Were you to ask me to identify the one thing necessary to get your idea, your passion, your solution off the ground, I would tell you this: you need to find your cheerleader. Taking risks, stepping out of bounds—like I did, like many I met during the Journey had done—is scary and lonely and can cut you off from some of your friends. It happened for me, and almost everyone I met mentioned it in their interviews. But as the popular Paulo Coelho quote floating around Facebook these days says, "When someone leaves, it's because someone else is about to arrive." Be prepared for the departures and open the door for those who will come in and support you, help you, and encourage you to continue down the path.

That person who just popped into your head—go ahead and write their name down here.

Chapter 6
I learned to see people

At one point, the journalist on the board of the 50 in 52 Journey told me that the hardest thing I would need to learn was how to listen. I paid close attention to this, but I found I was actually an excellent listener and had been practicing the art of listening my whole life. What I had not realized was that I did not know how to see people.

Learning to see people was one of the greatest lessons of this Journey. Seeing people through their eyes led me on a path straight to their hearts. Each one of us has dreams and hopes inside of us, but not all of us have the encouragement to live out those dreams. So many marginalized and poor people, in our very own country, feel they have no right to dream.

An unforgettable video was developed for the hospital baby shower program at the public hospital I worked for before the Journey. This hospital served 85 percent of Denver's indigent population. Of the thousands of babies born there, too many were born into the toughest of situations: in poverty, to single parents, as products of rape, or to parents who were imprisoned. None of these is the fault of the baby.

To give these little guys a good start in the first couple weeks of life, the hospital's foundation has worked for many years to provide bags with everything the babies need once they leave the safety and relative comfort of the hospital. Many times, that includes things like cribs and strollers, along with clothing, diapers, and other necessities.

The video was developed as a fundraising tool. It showed a child in an incubator in the NICU, born prematurely to a woman who had lost her job, was homeless, and had little education. The mother spoke proudly and directly to the camera, dreaming about the bright future her son would have. He would be smart and have a good job and would be happy. Each time I watched the video, I sobbed. I felt certain that a bright future would be tough for this child to come by, yet here was his mother, willing a positive future for him. Don't we all wish for that? Although she could not see it, she believed that one day it would happen.

I know what it means to be poor. I don't like to think about it. I was only eight when my mother had to make that choice between milk, orange juice, or shoes. I remember the welfare line. My mother did everything she could for us. She sacrificed so much. It was a short period in my life, only three years, but I will never forget it. I still can't write about it without crying.

So many people helped my family during this dark period. My brothers and I went away to summer camp. We went to private school. We did not go hungry. My mother knew where to look for help, and she swallowed her pride to get it. I found so many on my Journey who did not have the benefit of a woman like my mother in their lives.

Dallas was the first place I went where I had to deal head on with my fear of homeless people. A fear, a prejudice, that I did not know I had. I was heading to my interview with Larry Sykes with the Community Voice Mail program. Larry had completed a career in

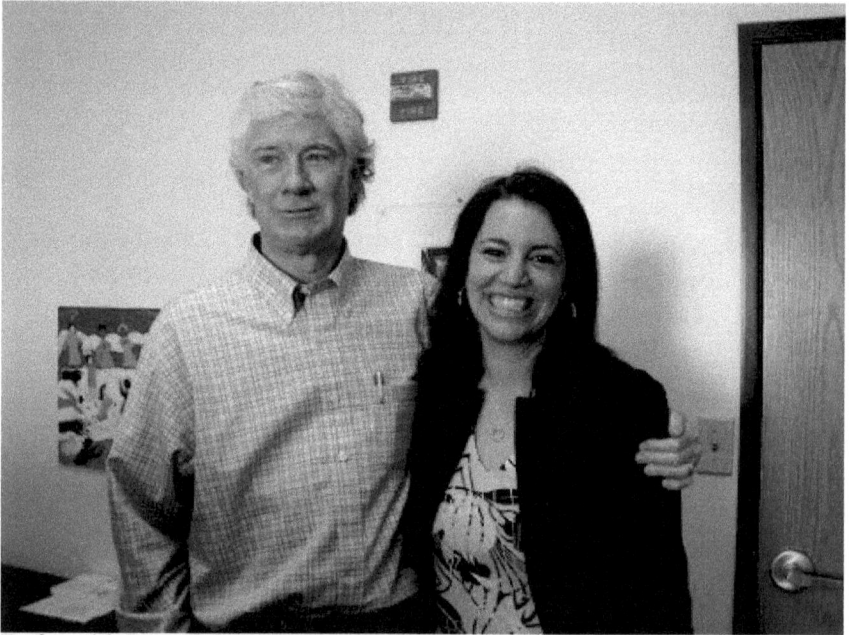

Dafna with Larry Sykes

business. One afternoon, while hanging out in his backyard barbecuing with friends, he had the epiphany that to truly help homeless people connect with jobs and (even more important to Larry) with their families; they needed a way to receive voicemail messages. Looking at Larry's tall, lean frame and shocking white crown of hair, I could see him controlling the boardroom. Yet, as he described his recent triumph—one of his homeless clients receiving the first communication in several years from his estranged daughter—he crumbled into tears before my eyes.

Larry's program was situated in the same building as a popular soup kitchen. As I walked toward the building from the parking garage, I noticed a large group of homeless men gathered about fifty feet from the entrance. I literally stopped in place. My brain instantly started sounding warning signals.

I remember thinking to myself at that moment, "How dare I stop in fear? I am on their turf, and I am here to talk about services provided to these people, and yet I stop in fear?" I was only four states into the Journey, and I admonished myself: if I could not have the presence of self to respectfully walk through this group of men, then I was not going to be able to accomplish this Journey. I took a deep breath, and as I walked through the group, they wished me a good morning. I wished them a good morning in return and entered the facility.

During the Journey, I met people all over the country who were providing services to homeless individuals, from Texas to Indiana to Nevada, and each was doing their work in different ways. Many had come from backgrounds in business or law—successful careers unrelated to serving the needs of the poor—and yet they each found their own way of making a difference. Bringing humanity to the way people who are homeless are treated was at the core of all the services I heard about.

The issue of homelessness is directly connected to experiences that formed me as a young woman making decisions about my life. It was when I was fourteen years old, that year when so much of my identity crystalized, that I first wrestled with the concept of homelessness and the lack of a solution. I would sit on the school bus each day, riding through once-majestic areas of Cincinnati. I'd stare out the window as large mansions and historic apartment buildings with detailed architecture, reflecting the grandeur of their time, flew by, but now the buildings were all run down and the neighborhoods blighted.

As the bus would exit that part of town and head for downtown Cincinnati, I remember seeing vacant warehouse after vacant warehouse. I knew homelessness was a problem in Cincinnati, and I knew

I had the answer. Fill these warehouses with beds and services. Teach people how to get jobs. Give people a clean, safe place to sleep. It seemed so simple to me.

During the 1980s in American life, families routinely watched TV while eating dinner. Our family was no different. Dinner often coincided with the local NBC evening news. I had a favorite newscaster who always seemed to connect the dots when it came to what was happening in the news and why it was important to how we lived our lives. I hung on his every word.

One day, it seemed he just disappeared from the newscast. No explanation as far as I can recall, just gone. Then a month later, he resurfaced. He had been living undercover on the streets of Cincinnati as a homeless man, with a camera embedded in his clothing. He reprimanded all the people of Cincinnati as he showed us how we "looked through" our homeless community. He told us we would never fix this problem unless we began to look at, and truly see, those experiencing homelessness as people who are as important as you or I.

I was transfixed. I knew then that I was guilty of looking through people. Only during this Journey, some twenty years later, would I finally learn how to see.

It is a funny thing when you look back and reflect on who your greatest influencers were when the lessons finally sink in. My teacher, in this instance, this newscaster? Jerry Springer. I guess we each have our moments of brilliance.

With each new state I visited, I found that when I met people tackling homelessness, they were unique in their methods. One element, however, was the same: it came down to seeing the individual, not the label. In Lexington, Kentucky, I met Judy Ramsey and Ginny McLaughlin, the codirectors and cofounders of the Catholic Action Center. Judy and Ginny were coming at the issue from the faith perspective. With the hundreds of faith-based organizations that existed in Kentucky, not to mention secular organizations working to tackle the problems of homelessness, they could not fathom how homelessness could possibly continue to exist in Kentucky. Yet it did.

Judy and Ginny took a hard look at the problems and determined that there were many contributing factors. Many people thought that

Dafna with Judy Ramsey and Ginny McLaughlin

by feeding the hungry, they would solve the problem. But Judy and Ginny learned that food was only one of many basic necessities that homeless individuals lacked. Many homeless people don't have a place they can go to the bathroom. Yes, feeding these people is important, but so is hygiene and dignity. Those were being overlooked.

For Judy and Ginny, the path began with opening a hospitality house where needs of hunger and needs of cleanliness could be addressed. From there, the project grew and grew. Their first step was seeing individuals and treating them as they would like to be treated.

What does seeing people mean to you? Are there people you pass in the hustle and bustle of an ordinary day and never truly see? Are there people sitting on a street corner whose gaze you cross the street to avoid?

Are you able to move beyond lumping individuals together so you can see the challenge that is truly most important to solve? This is the key. The people I met on my Journey answered this question. They learned to see people deeply. They learned to walk a mile in the other's shoes. After all, many of them began in those very same shoes.

Chapter 7
I found women

Of the people I interviewed during the Journey, 65 percent were women. Women have always played a powerful role in my life. As a young teen, I joined my first "segregated" organization. By "segregated," I mean the boys' and girls' groups worked separately to plan programs and events. Although there were often combined programs, I enjoyed the energy of working in an all-female environment. I chose to attend an all-female college. I found many opportunities to head uptown to our brother campus, but I enjoyed the learning and opportunities that being among women gave me.

I chose a career in nonprofit management, following my personal mission of not complaining about a problem unless I was willing to work on the solution. Once again I surrounding myself, if not completely, then largely, with women. As my career advanced, I chose to become involved with Hadassah, which has the largest female membership of any nonprofit organization in the United States. Once again, as in my youth, I was surrounded by powerful, opinionated, and action-oriented women.

I relish the role these experiences have played in shaping how I think, how I drive my career, and how I raise my daughter and son.

Hours of driving America's highways and country roads allowed for lots of reflection time. As I drove through the beautiful state of Wyoming, I caught myself in deep thought about the people I was meeting. There were so many women. Women, in all corners of the country, doing work not only to help their own families but to help those around them who were also in need of support. In rural parts of the country, I also marveled at the number of Jewish women I was meeting in places that I did not think had any Jewish population to speak of. Indeed, on my trip to Lander, Wyoming, I was going to meet a woman who was the one Jewish person in the entire city.

I worried that perhaps my referral pool was too small. But at this point, most of my Jewish friends were not yet on Facebook. None of them were on Twitter. And I had been using the incredible Help a Reporter Out resource, which casts a very wide net. Perhaps these women appeared on my path to teach me something about my own life.

Linda Barton was a transplant to Wyoming from Los Angeles. Her tall, lean frame, long, coiffed brown hair, sparkling brown eyes, and stylish business attire easily gave away her cosmopolitan background. She had met and fallen in love with a man from Lander. When she moved there to set up her new life, she learned there was a big discrepancy between the after-school hours and when parents got home from work. There was nothing for kids to do. Unsupervised kids were getting hurt, avoiding their homework, and committing petty crimes.

After leaving a career in finance, Linda felt she could help the kids and families of Lander by opening Lights on Lander, a program to help kids with homework and provide access to after-school activities, like Tae Kwon Do. The crime rate went down, as did emergency room visits, and home-

Lights on Lander

work completion and test grades went up. Lights on Lander is now a federally funded program. Linda, an outsider who fully embraced her new home, set the children of Lander down a path toward success.

The women I met on the Journey also gave me insight into an entirely new level of strength.

I was blessed with the gift of bearing children from my womb. I don't take lightly that it was a gift not necessarily guaranteed. I cherish my role as mother, and I cherish the children whose souls became a part of my world. I am grateful. I have friends and family members who chose not to have children or were otherwise unable, and I have friends who never found partners with whom to start a family. A small part inside of me has always been sad for those who wanted children, but it wasn't to be. These were brilliant women, beautiful women, and loving women. I knew that if these women could bring children into the world, those children would be spectacular. The Journey taught me that to love a child and rear a child, and indeed, to create a fabulous human being, does not require the use of your own womb.

Now, I don't want to give you the wrong idea. I certainly thought that was possible, and Michael and I talked early on of our shared dream of adopting a child in the future. One Journey day in Florida solidified our dream.

Cherie, Tricia, and Karen. Three very different women giving life and love to children they did not bear. Cherie Adkins was a captain with the Tampa Police Department. If you did not know better, you could mistake Cherie for the cheerleader next door, all grown up, energetic smile and long blond hair included. In fact, Cherie is a no-nonsense woman who handles some of the Tampa Police Department's toughest calls. She is often the one to comfort families who must deal with news of the death or severe injury of a loved one.

Dafna with Cherie Adkins

Cherie did not have children her husband's children became her love, and when her grandbaby was diagnosed with leukemia, she brought her department together to raise money to fight for medical support. She showed me the strength of true love.

Tricia Harrold and her husband were devastated when they discovered they could not have children of their own. Determined to love, and to mother, she, along with her husband, opened their

Dafna with Tricia Harrold

home to foster children. She adopted three and then went on to foster over fifty children. Tricia, a tall woman with short blond hair, who has warmth in her being and parental love emanating from her face, is now "retired" and continues to help children born to others who are in crisis. She volunteers for an emergency shelter, helping kids through the scariest moments of being separated from family to being brought to a safe haven.

Tricia showed me that life does not go as planned, but that is no reason not to seek other paths to fulfilling your purpose.

Karen Saeks is a lovely woman with shoulder-length blond hair, bleached from long days in the Florida sun. Her no-nonsense expression easily melts away when she wears a loving smile. In her retirement, Karen became distressed by the living conditions of the nearby children of migrant workers. Starting by recruiting neighbors and friends, Karen organized a program to provide the children with everything they'd need for being tucked in at night: pajamas, books, a blanket, a pillow, and a stuffed animal.

Dafna with Karen Saeks and friends

The more Karen learned about the needs of the children and their families, the more items she collected. She was driven by the fact that the migrant families lived so close to people blessed with much affluence, and they had nothing. Karen has "adopted" her migrant neighbors.

When I met her, she was collecting clothes, housewares, and food for every member of a migrant worker's family. As I interviewed a family that Karen's program supports, they told me they call her their "angel."

These women, whom I met over the span of twenty-four hours and several hundreds of miles, showed me an unconditional love for children who did not come out of their wombs but were connected to their souls. I look forward to the time when I may bring a gift like that to a child. When you give love to a child, whether or not you birthed that child, you give a gift to the world.

The lessons I learned from women went beyond those of nurturing and mothering. From the women I met, I learned about drive, about rising to the top against all odds, about power that is pulled from deep inside, and about faith.

Women are notorious for failing to own their power. We often fail to call ourselves experts in any arena. Perhaps this behavior comes from years of being bred to play a supporting role? Today, many leadership programs geared toward women teach how to stand up and proclaim your strengths, instead of hiding your gifts behind a veil of modesty or a fear of being called a braggart.

In Massachusetts, I met a woman named Christa Drew. How to describe Christa? Her energy just emanated determination, drive, and

Dafna interviewing Christa Drew

a certain air of refusing to be defeated. Her passion was social justice, and Christa told me she believes hunger is the root of social injustice. Keep a person hungry, and they cannot rise above their lot. Christa has found many ways to work on her passion. She is committed to working to the point of achieving a solution worthy of a Nobel Peace Prize.

I remember when Christa uttered the words "Nobel Peace Prize." I was caught off guard. Yes, I had heard people tell me they wanted to put an end to things like hunger, violence, and poverty. I had never heard one person aim to achieve at so high a level. I pondered why.

As 2009 went on, I continually thought back to the people I had met. I thought about Christa when I received my first television coverage. The first comment I received, which appeared to come from a woman, said, "Who does she think she is?"

There it is, ladies and gentlemen, plain as day. Our society punishes people who step out and name their goals. We call people who work for good, and receive recognition for it, selfish, lofty, and self-important. Christa seemed unfazed by claiming her goal out loud. She taught me to stand tall and to openly declare my goals, then hunker down and do the work to achieve them.

I learned about women climbing to the top against all odds. Not with a particular path in mind—simply with the goals to learn more and do more. Dr. Joycelyn Elders reminded me so much of my

Dafna with Dr. Joycelyn Elders

grandmother. She was an impeccably dressed woman of color with a short stature but mighty force. Dr. Elders grew up in Arkansas picking cotton. She wanted to attend college to become a clerk in a department store. The United Methodist Women sent her to college. Her brothers and sisters picked cotton to pay for her bus fare. While in college at Philander Smith in Little Rock, she heard a black female doctor speak. She had no idea that black people could become doctors, let alone that women could become doctors.

Dr. Elders believes that "you can't be what you can't see." She worked her way through school and then the army, using her GI Bill to attend medical school. Ultimately, she became the surgeon general under President Bill Clinton. Today she works to be that role model for other women, just as her role model had inspired her.

She didn't have a master plan, but when she got her goals in her sights, she set forth to achieve them, one step, one goal at a time. She says she came from what we might call "nothing." I would argue that she came from everything, because she had the support of her family. And for her, it is not enough that she has achieved the highest level of medical respect. Dr. Elders is there for other young women. She makes herself available to speak and to mentor. She taught me that to help another, I must let them see my success and envision themselves achieving that success. Then I must hold their hands while they get there.

I also learned from a number of young women to remember what it feels like to believe you can accomplish whatever you set your mind to.

In Texas, two high school students recounted the destruction and devastation of Hurricane Katrina. They had been only a bus ride away from the aftermath and were itching to help. When I arrived at their Houston home for the interview, Marissa Katz and Shoshana Yaffee had just

Dafna with Marissa Katz and Shoshana Yaffee

returned from basketball practice and were still in their uniforms. They had long hair and giggled frequently. As I looked at them, I saw a whisper of what I may have been like at that age with my best friend. I didn't have to look too hard, as I was spending that night in the home of my college roommate, Mirit. There had been no end of giggling as we "studied" in New York together.

Dafna and Mirit

The two girls were no strangers to serving the community. Both were raised in homes where helping others was expected. The girls came by their activities quite naturally. Marissa and Shoshana started by reaching out to their friends who volunteered with them in the community pantry. They then went to their school and told the administration about their plan. They were going to raise money to rent a bus and take whoever wanted to join them to New Orleans where they would help in the massive cleanup effort.

The girls' actions may not seem like such an amazing thing in light of how many other people found ways to come together and assist. Yet, these two girls set their sights on a goal of supporting people they did not know, whom they would probably never meet. It did not matter to them. They saw a need, and they wanted to fill it. Their teachers did not tell them to do it. Their parents did not tell them to do it. Together, they decided to be part of the solution. Together, they gathered their peers and the adults in their lives. Together, they built a community and solved a problem.

They were so nonchalant in the interview. They knew what they had done was good, but they certainly did not think it was extraordinary.

How can we all harness those days of sixteen or seventeen? How can we see a path or a need and simply take the steps needed to make it happen? With every passing year of our personal journeys, we add layers of what we see as complications. Life happens, work gets busy, there may be children or aging parents to care for. What if these are not complications, but rather the foundations of our team and our training?

I want to close this section by telling you about a few women who taught me the power of following your beliefs.

Alisha Whiteway of Raleigh, North Carolina, was a dynamic woman, larger than life, with her energy and electric presence. Alisha followed her dreams to the US Army, where she was trained as a broadcast journalist. Ten years and many experiences in war-torn areas of the

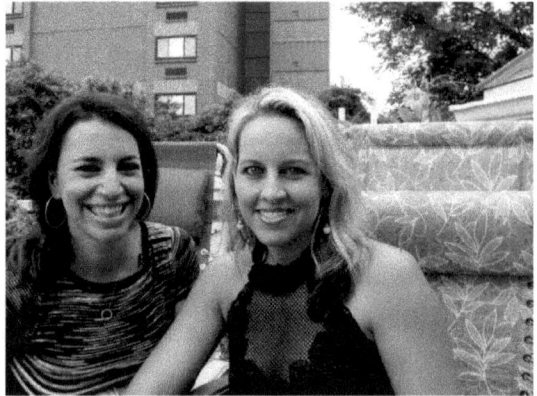

Dafna with Alisha Whiteway

globe later, Alisha retired as an officer and began to examine what she wanted to do to continue contributing to the country.

Alisha tried her hand at conventional broadcast journalism, but she found that the work drained her energy, as she was only meeting people at the lowest points in their lives. Knowing that she had a gift for sharing stories, and marrying that with her desire to show the best in people, she began her own online network that told the stories of people making the world a better place. Through her work, which was similar to the Journey, Alisha discovered that sharing inspiring stories of those making a positive impact in the community could elevate others and add value to viewer's lives every day.

And then there was Joan Stewart in West Virginia. A small woman with neat, short hair cut in a classic bob and a vibrant smile, Joan was happily going about her life as a banker. She sat in church one day and felt a particular calling to join the ministry. Now, you may be thinking, "Doesn't this story belong in the section on faith?" Well, maybe, but what Joan really taught me was about listening to instinct and blazing a new trail while following the path.

Dafna with Joan Stewart

Joan did not simply listen to the message she heard and take leave of her banking career. No, she challenged G-d. "OK, G-d" she said aloud. "If you want me to join the ministry, you help me pass the test. I'm not studying." Well, she passed the test.

Joan kept up her end of the deal. She packed up her life to move back to the area of West Virginia from which she hailed. Her work at her church has elevated the community and West Virginia. Her church has become a destination of choice for college students seeking to take a moment out of their lives to serve those in need. The visiting students do things like repairing homes and digging drainage ditches. Many people in this area live in conditions that many Americans do not realize exist in our country.

I like to think that each morning as I prepare for the day, I put on my costume for the job at hand. Yes, some of it is in my closet, and some is in my makeup collection, but most of what I wear comes from those I met on my Journey. I wear courage. I wear power. I wear love. These women and so many others armed me. As Dr. Elders taught us, "You can't be it if you can't see it." In those words, she summed up the purpose of my Journey and the journey I still have ahead.

Chapter 8
I found that age doesn't matter

Age is such a curious thing. Each year, as my birthday passes, I look in the mirror and think I can see my younger self. Could I have possibly reached such a number? I don't feel *that* old. Does each new year allow us more opportunities? Does age determine limits on what we might accomplish?

As I headed off to tour the country I knew, I hoped I'd find a diverse population, but I never even thought about age. In Ohio, I would encounter both my oldest and my youngest representations of people solving problems in their communities.

The oldest person I met was ninety-one-year-old Alfred Tibor. A Holocaust survivor, he was short and frail, but, as I would see in many people I met, neither of those descriptors implies weakness. Alfred spent the entirety of the war in a Siberian labor camp. During his imprisonment, he had no idea what was going on in the outside world, and he was angry—very angry.

Each day, he would fantasize about getting into a tank, driving it to his community, and opening fire on them for

Dafna with Alfred Tibor

abandoning him to the hell he was living. Upon his liberation, he packed up his anger and headed for home, only to find complete destruction. He could find no remnants of his life before the war. As he learned about the fate of his community, his anger did not grow—it crumbled.

In a moment of recognizing his family and community's complete destruction, he realized that the anger he harbored, and the revenge that had fueled him, made him no better than the perpetrators of the single most heinous crime against humanity our world had ever seen. He vowed not to live in anger and resentment.

Alfred came to America, started a family, and began living the American dream. One day, while Alfred sat in synagogue, his rabbi declared they had raised funds to build a memorial to the millions who perished in the Holocaust.

Alfred stood up and said to his adult son, "I will be the sculptor." His son looked back at him and said, "Dad, you are not a sculptor." Before he was imprisoned, Alfred had wanted to be a sculptor. In this moment, he realized he could recapture the dreams of his youth and learn the trade he had once built his life's plans around.

As he perfected his craft, Alfred realized he would be able to make a true impact on the world by sculpting images that captured the qualities of joy, love, and life. He has crafted sculptures of mothers holding their babies aloft as he works to recapture what it might have felt like as his own mother held him. This feeling is only a memory for Alfred, as he and his mother were separated during the war, and he lost her to the Nazi Holocaust. His sculptures contain movement in the form of ballerinas, to show flow and love. They feature red balloons to show joy and innocence.

As Alfred explains to audiences that listen to his story, only through living a life full of love and joy could he truly beat the Nazis at their own game.

Not only did Alfred survive, he thrived.

My youngest interviewee was Ashley Young in Batavia, Ohio. At fourteen years old, Ashley was at the height of her embarrassing adolescent years. At this age, she probably looked in the mirror and criticized the roundness of her face and the color of her eyes. But I saw a shy, striking beauty in the way she wore her black hair pulled back and the gentle strokes with which she had applied youthful makeup to large, captivating eyes. I'm sure the last thing she expected on the day I met her was a stranger greeting her at her school bus stop and asking for an interview.

Dafna with Ashley Young

I had come to Batavia to visit the Stepping Stones residential facility for adults with profound physical and mental disabilities. I had planned to interview Ashley's mom, who lives on-site and runs the day-to-day programming for the residents. When I finished the interview, her mom said, "It's not me you need to interview. You have to meet my daughter."

When she said this, I immediately thought of my own daughter, of whom I am so proud. I could not deny her request. I stood at Ashley's bus stop, awkwardly imagining the police stopping to ask me what I was doing, stalking kids coming home from school. When she arrived, Ashley looked confused as to why I knew about her story, but she agreed to speak with me.

I sat with Ashley in an outdoor amphitheater on the Stepping Stones grounds. We sat on logs, surrounded by the dense beauty of the Ohio landscape. Trees towering forty feet in the air around us created a canopy of deep green beauty. I asked her to tell me her story.

"I go to school each day and my friends are always using the word 'retarded.' They'll trip in the hall and call themselves 'retarded,' or they'll do something klutzy and their friends will call them 'retarded,' and it really bothers me."

Ashley works with her mother. She hangs out in the pool, and on the outdoor nature courses, with the Stepping Stones residents. To her, they are not "retarded." And whenever her friends used that word, she felt they were being disrespectful to the residents even though they did not know them. The Stepping Stones residents certainly did not hear the young students speaking that way.

She decided she had to do something about it. She went to her room and put together a CD slideshow of the Stepping Stones residents. Ashley told their story, emphasizing that her friends had never done anything to disrespect another person. But even though they might not realize it, when they used the word "retarded," they were sending a message of disrespect to her Stepping Stones friends, who were like family to her, as well as to others with disabilities.

Ashley didn't know what she would do with the CD. She showed it to a teacher, who then showed it to the principal, who then asked Ashley to do an assembly. Ashley was scared, but she thought she might be able to make a difference, so she did it. Then word got out, and other schools wanted Ashley to come. Time and again, Ashley summoned the confidence she needed to move forward and tell her story.

The newspapers wrote about Ashley. The impact she made continued long after that day when she closed her bedroom door and dreamed about how she might make a difference.

Ashley and Alfred are two relatively private people who witnessed discrimination, and worse. For Alfred, the atrocities were direct. For Ashley, the discrimination was directed at her friends. Both decided that they could not stand by and let it continue.

Alfred could not let negativity win. He taught himself a craft and mastered that craft. He could have chosen to reflect his grief through his work, but he did not. To him, his sculptures are a chance to bring his truths to light: that there is joy in love, there is peace in kindness, there is a future in recognizing those who are different from you. Make no mistake; Alfred is waging a war with his work. His war is against ignorance and bigotry.

Ashley is doing the same. It may seem simple to create a CD of images. It may seem simple to ask one's peers to be a bit more aware of the language they use. But, I ask you this: do you remember four teen? I do. Fourteen years old is not exactly a time in most of our lives when we have the courage to shake things up. Yes, her initial steps were simple, but her follow-through was mighty.

No, age does not matter. As you look in the mirror each year, do not ask yourself if you notice a wrinkle, a pimple, or some gray hair. Ask yourself instead, "What is it that I am no longer willing to tolerate this year?" Whether you are fourteen, forty, or one hundred and four, take the power of Alfred and Ashley. Look in that mirror and see them cheering you on. Then say it out loud: "I've got this!"

Age simply does not matter. Deciding you want to change something in your life is the only thing that does.

Chapter 9
I found that size really does not matter

One of the most amazing things about driving far and wide, as I did on this Journey, was seeing each of the tiny towns along the way. As the nominations came in, I was worried I would mostly find myself in the major cities of each state, but that absolutely did not turn out to be the case. Sure, the Journey reached the big cities and towns, but it also found the tiny ones. I visited towns ranging in population from 78 in Dawn, Missouri, to 250 in Roslyn, South Dakota, to 3,500 in Huxley, Iowa, to 8.3 million in New York, New York.

Each town has its own character and unique set of problems. The people of each town have their own language and their own sets of desires. What I found was this: the smaller the town, the stronger the opinions.

I left St. Louis, Missouri (population 2.87 million) for Dawn, Missouri, having spent the previous day meeting people from around St. Louis who had never even heard of such a town. The drive was about four and a half hours, and, as could be predicted, my sidekick and navigator, Betty the GPS, decided to stop working as soon as she took me off the main road.

About four states into the Journey, I figured out that my BlackBerry GPS was simply not going to cut it. It was hard to drive safely and look at the screen. The BlackBerry GPS was not a speaking system, so I dug into the ever-emptying bank account and bought myself a stand-alone GPS. I hoped it would get me where I needed to go while allowing me the luxury of watching the road.

I found myself on a sign-free dirt road with approximately five miles to go until I reached my destination. As Betty continued to flash "recalculating route," I switched over to my phone GPS system and entered "Dawn."

Should you happen to wind up on the road that passes through Dawn, you might notice nothing except that the speed limit changes from sixty-five to thirty-five as you fly by. You might be through in a blink, and well on your way to your next town or the next stretch of sixty-five-mile-per-hour country highway roads. I was excited to stop in Dawn; I had passed by so many towns like it during the year, and always wondered what it might be like to meet the people who lived there.

As you come into town, there is a small restaurant and retail shop with a single old-style gasoline pump on your left. A bit further up the road on the right is a small, worn-looking post office. By the best guesses of the Dawn residents I met, seventy-eight people make up Dawn's population. I met with the people who were trying to keep the town from disappearing.

The Café Group ranged in age from middle-aged to seniors. Their features, some rugged and others more citylike, reflected a mix of what you might see all over America. Mark Sykes and his wife, Teresa, owned the Daybreak Café on Main Street. Patricia Weaver's family had run the café before them. Another member, Marc Anderson, grew up in Dawn, and after an illustrious career in the aircraft industry, he returned from San Francisco with his wife, Johanne Blackburn, to enjoy retirement in the community he remembered so fondly.

As we sat chatting in the café, a group of men were enjoying their morning ritual of breakfast, coffee, and catching up before they headed out to work their land. The shop and café have been around for as long as anyone can remember; Marc even remembers a time half a century ago when the town had some bustle to it. As the years went on, the town kept its regular slow pace while the world kept whizzing by, catching most of the children who grew up there in its rush.

Today, the town is quiet. No one has moved here in many years, and quite frankly, the group is not sure that anyone not originally from the area would be all that comfortable. The Daybreak Café has required a significant amount of hard work, and instead of adding to the Sykes family's income, continuing to keep it open comes at a personal financial loss. When the group began to meet, they believed it was the one thing preventing the town from dying.

Trying to figure out ways to keep towns vital and alive is a struggle across small-town America, and it is no different in Dawn. The residents hold open meetings, and everyone in town shows up to ensure their opinion is heard. There is fear from some who just don't want the town to get too big. There are some who are leery of strangers coming in and disrupting their lifestyle. Then there are those like the Café Group who would like to see the town stay more or less the same, while still growing enough to sustain the families who live there and their small-town way of life.

Slowly, the group was making headway. The Friday fish fry at the café was a big draw, bringing people to Dawn from neighboring towns, twenty or so miles away, for a lively evening of family fun.

Reaching out to the children who grew up in these small towns has been another way to work on revitalization. Those who are starting families can come home and raise their children away from some of the safety concerns of raising a child in the city. Patricia hoped her daughter would return to Dawn after her son-in-law completed his US military service.

I left Dawn knowing that the Café Group had an uphill battle, perhaps a little more uphill than it would be in a larger town. Yet the spirit of the people working to save the café, and ultimately the town, is strong.

While the community in Dawn was fighting for the town's existence, the community in Roslyn, South Dakota, found themselves fighting to be acknowledged in the first place. One of the challenges (or some may say blessings) of living in a small town is that the place may not show up on a map. This was the situation in Roslyn, South Dakota.

To establish their identity, the town had brought in consultant after consultant with no success. One day, Lawrence Diggs, a tall, stately black man with an aura of authority and a flair for the creative, moved to town and convinced the townspeople that a Vinegar Museum would be their ticket to success.

Dafna with Lawrence Diggs

Lawrence is a vinegar expert. He had searched for four years to find a small town where he could escape the rush of San Francisco and concentrate on his writing. After a four-year search, his realtor led him to Roslyn. With Lawrence's arrival, Roslyn experienced diversity for the first time in the town's known history. To his pleasure (and a bit of surprise), he was welcomed into the community, and he has been part of its fiber since his arrival.

As I learned on this trip, rural America is facing a dire end. As children complete their education, they are finding opportunities in other cities and leaving the smaller towns of their childhood. Rural South Dakota is facing a decline in population, income, and opportunity. The people of Roslyn have come together, with Lawrence often leading the conversation, trying to figure out how to bring people and opportunity to Roslyn.

After many experts failed them, the town's people pointed to Lawrence. And thus, the International Vinegar Museum was born. Roslyn is now literally and figuratively on the map—every map!

Another small-town challenge, which Roslyn also faced, occurs when people from outside come into your small town and think they know what is best for your community. What this Journey has shown me very clearly is that only

The International Vinegar Museum

you, in your community, in your day-to-day life, truly know the challenges you are facing and the right way to solve them. Sometimes it takes a little creativity, and sometimes you need to build up your forces to protect what you hold dear.

To me, roadside barns have always been a place of mystery and impending adventure. Along Kansas Highway 15, in the town of Dexter, is the Stone Barn Mercantile. Inside this beautiful barn is a treasure trove of fun local finds, and there are endless stories of passersby peeking inside the mysterious place. It was a group of passersby thinking they could "fix" Dexter, and surrounding towns, that, without meaning to, caused the mercantile and the ABCDE Group to come into existence.

Dafna with Shannon, Roger, and Carol

Shannon Martin, a young mother with shoulder-length light-brown hair and a medium-sized frame, is the mercantile's proprietor. She holds a fountain of entrepreneurial energy and vision.

The passersby determined that the rural Kansas area needed a recreational lake to help create economic prosperity. The lake would have taken out much of the town's fields, including the farms behind what is now the mercantile. The towns people were concerned. They liked the idea of greater riches, but not at the cost of their land.

Shannon, along with Roger and Carol Black's longtime Kansas family and other dedicated townspeople, came together. They brought in the towns of Atlanta, Burden, Cambridge, and Dexter (A, B, C, and D) to create a group of dedicated people to share ideas and build their own prosperity.

The energy was powerful in the meeting, and ideas flew and grew. One idea led to the creation of a new farming tool, and a factory was soon built. Another idea was to create the Stone Barn Mercantile. All the projects brought attention and money to the area.

The ABCDE Group (the "E" stands for everybody) will not rest. They have tasted success and will continue to bond together to increase the region's success so their children, grandchildren, and great-grandchildren may continue to live on and prosper from the land.

Barn Mercantile

Solving problems in a small town or small community poses a unique set of challenges. Let's start simply enough: How many people are available to come together? What histories and personalities are gathered? Is it possible to look beyond the past and work together? It is almost certain, when you live in a small town, that challenges faced by one town are faced by many.

The people I met in small towns had to think the most creatively of any place I visited. Each person had to find new ways to use old resources. They had to stretch well beyond their comfort zones to find solutions that fit the challenge. Everyone benefited from the result.

Whether you live in a small town or not, consider what part of your challenge can benefit from small-town thinking. No, size doesn't matter. The number of people you hope to impact does. Start with one—yourself—and take it from there.

Inside Barn Mercantile

Chapter 10
I found love . . .

You probably thought this section would be all about my Michael. Wait for it, we'll get there, but love takes so many unbelievable forms. Having really been new to love when I embarked on this Journey, I saw it everywhere.

Love of neighbor.

Once on a flight to, well, somewhere (you know, I can't remember where I was flying to on that particular trip, but I took a minimum of two flights a week), I met a Bible salesman. He had just completed a trip to Colorado Springs to showcase some of his new Bibles and faith-based romance novels. He struck up a conversation as I took my seat. I always loved airplane conversations because I knew that with my life being as it was, any conversation could lead to an interview and a new story to share.

Phil was a tall, thin man with short, neat dark hair and glasses. I couldn't help thinking as I looked at him that he could play the part of Waldo if *Where's Waldo?* ever became a movie. As I began asking him about his life, I learned he was Mennonite who, at a young age, had taken a mission trip to Haiti. As he spoke, I could hear his passion for his faith and for service, and I was intrigued about where this conversation could go.

After his first stint in Haiti, he came home and married Emily. Emily was a beautiful woman with the face of a girl. She had long, straight-edged brown hair. She wore plain clothes as her religion dictated, but with a hint of style showing the flare and energy she brought to her life. Phil's heart, now bound to Emily, was also deeply connected to Haiti in ways he was not sure he understood. He felt at home in the land and with its people. After the wedding, Phil and his bride moved to Haiti for an extended mission trip.

Times were exceptionally tough in Haiti. A young teenage girl who was pregnant with twins lived in the neighboring home. The parents of the pregnant girl approached Phil and Emily and begged them to adopt the babies and bring them to the United States. Although barely adults themselves, Phil and Emily were eager to help, but they knew there would be many barriers to achieving this goal. The twins were born, and Phil and Emily fell deeply in love. They jumped every hurdle, getting the blessings of the family's tribal leader and following every painstaking legal step to bring the girls home.

There was one hurdle perhaps they had not thought of. When they returned to their family's strictly Mennonite community, there would be no people of color for the girls to see and identify with. Loving their children, and wanting them to know they were not the only people with dark skin, Phil and Emily moved from their Mennonite enclave to a mixed-race neighborhood. The move was a big challenge for a devout couple so accustomed to being surrounded by family, and with help never too far away.

As Phil shared his story with me, I was completely engrossed. The love, the dedication, the bond he and Emily shared in their passion and their faith—it was movie quality for me. But this was not the story he wanted to tell me. He was giving me background for the real story.

Emily homeschooled her three girls in their new home—her adopted twins, with their rich brown skin, hair in braids, and the plump bodies of young children preparing to grow, and her biological daughter, who was younger, thinner, with paper-white skin and shoulder-length ash-blond hair. One day, while Emily was teaching a lesson and cooking dinner (multitasking as every mother must at one time or another), one of the twins went upstairs, curious about what was being prepared. She was barely six years old. She pulled a step stool over to the stove and climbed up to peer into the pot of bubbling water on the burner. As she reached up, she grabbed the handle of the pot and slipped. Scalding hot water spilled over her body.

Emily heard the shrieks and came running. She called 911. Her badly burned daughter was rushed to the hospital, and doctors began the painful procedure of treating the wound.

Dafna, Phil, Emily, and their family

As she sat with her daughter, Emily remembered her Amish grandfather once used a salve that the Amish had created to treat serious burns. She put out a call for help in the Amish community. Within a short period, she received a call from a family whose members were practitioners of this treatment. They would house Phil and Emily and their daughters while they treated the patient. Emily checked her daughter out of the hospital and off they went.

Phil had shared his story with me not because he thought I'd be interested in buying his wares, but because he wanted me to know about this family who saved his daughter. The Amish treatment prevented her from the serious scarring that traditional hospital treatment would have left behind on her dark brown skin, which had turned a pale pink from the burn. This family did not know Emily and Phil. They did not agree to treat them only because they were Mennonite. They helped because their love for people superseded their own needs.

As we came in for a landing, I gave Phil my email address. Not knowing whether this Amish family had email access, he said he would try to put me in touch. I waited and waited until one day an email came from the Amish family. They had agreed to meet me and tell their story.

When the day came to meet Steven and Eunice Slabaugh at their home in McGaheysville, Virginia, I got very lost and ended up arriving late in the evening. Nine children, neatly dressed in plain clothes, simple white tops and muted color pants or skirts, and with their hair nicely combed, ranging in age from three to sixteen, sat quietly on the couch. Steven is a short man with a strong smile, a muscular frame, a head of brown hair, and a neat mustache. Eunice is about the same height as her husband, with long, neat hair and oversized glasses. Her glasses seemed to swallow her face, but they allowed me to see every expression of love and concern that flashed in her eyes as she spoke.

Dafna with Steven and Eunice Slabaugh

The children sat quietly through the interview. It was clear their parents did not feel that what they shared was extraordinary, but simply an ordinary story of service to others. All that was extraordinary to them was the severity of the little girl's burn.

To treat Phil and Emily's daughter, volunteers had to scour the forest for a specific leaf that was then deveined and boiled. The salve was made, and every hour, fresh leaves were coated in the salve to replace the ones from the previous leaf change. At the time of my interview with the Slabaughs, this system was being studied at Johns Hopkins. The Amish already knew the power of the treatment.

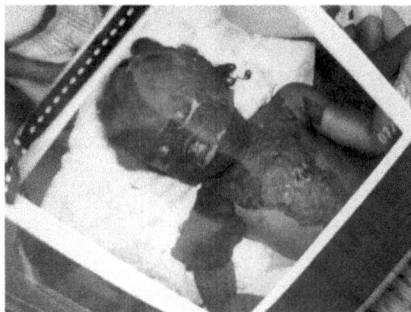

To keep the patient calm, the Slabaughs brought a harp into their home for their sixteen-year-old daughter to play for the six-year-old patient. The daughter was thin and blond; her face glowing with kindness and warmth. It

Phil and Emily's daughter

is against church doctrine to have musical instruments in your home. The Slabaughs were careful to respect their faith, but they also needed to keep the young girl calm and still. They did not ask for anything in return for their care and treatment; they did it because that is what you do when you love another.

As had been the case many times on my Journey, I did not have a place to sleep that night. Mr. Slabaugh offered to put me up in their trailer in the backyard. I had no cell signal and no way to let Michael know where I was. I experienced a "there are no atheists in foxholes" moment as I prayed for safety, though I was quite certain I could not find a safer place on earth.

I had to leave the Slabaugh home at three thirty the following morning to be on schedule for my next interview many hours' drive away. When I awoke, I found a sack of fresh blueberry muffins, fresh pumpkin bread, and fresh streusel loaf for me to take on my travels. Just as they had welcomed Phil and Emily's daughter, the Slabaughs welcomed me, and treated me with the most incredible love.

I feel the need to stop here for a moment. Love is such a trigger word. If you have it or are in it, love is wonderful. If you are denied it, or are desperately seeking it, love can be the most painful of words. At different points in my relationships, love has held so many varying levels of comfort or pain.

When my first marriage was failing and I would witness loving calls between my friends and their spouses, I would feel empty. I would watch movies portraying deep and passionate love, and I would sob with pain and envy. I wondered whether a love like that would ever exist for me.

Love was also complicated with my parents when I made choices they did not agree with. I loved them deeply and felt pain with equal depth. When I saw parent–child relationships that had a strong dynamic, I wondered how I too could have a family like that.

While traveling this country, I was in a deep, loving relationship and in a good place with my family. My eyes and my heart were open to see love without my own pain attached to it.

As you read my stories of love, please know that like other challenges you face, the love problem is one that can be solved, and solving it can benefit the community. I had to start by learning to love myself. I had to develop a relationship with myself. It took a bit of work to be able to look in the mirror and like the person in the reflection. This effort helped me to say "I deserve better" in all areas of my life. That step brought me further on my path to creating the life I want to live.

Chapter 11
Love for our struggling youth

As I traveled throughout the country, I was amazed at the impact men in particular are having on our youth. In Alaska, Florida, and Oklahoma, three men are changing the trajectory of our communities. All three had to first overcome their own varied life challenges. While they might not describe what they do as love, I don't know of any other force as powerful that would drive these men to make the sacrifices and take the risks they have.

Mao Tosi, a former NFL defensive end player, is a big man. At six foot six, he filled the space around me. Mao is Samoan, and his brown skin and full head of wild, curly hair radiate energy and life. Although Mao often wears his heart on his sleeve, a rare condition caused him to have not one but two heart attacks on the field, necessitating early retirement from his football career. His upbringing was rough and devoid of much parental interaction. When he went off to college, he begged his best friend to join him. His friend chose another path and ultimately ended up dying in a jail fight. Mao feels the pain of his friend's death every day. In Alaska, the state with the highest dropout rate in America, he tries to honor his friend's memory by connecting kids who have dropped out of school with their passions. He teaches them how they can make an income pursuing their passions and helps them earn a GED along the way.

Dafna and Mao Tosi and students

I learned about Mao while on a delayed, and then diverted, flight to Anchorage from Denver. The woman seated next to me lived in Anchorage, and she told me about Mao. She did not personally know him, but she looked up his number for me and suggested I give him a call. I was shocked when he answered the phone. I met him in a grocery store parking lot, where he had me leave my car and get into his large black SUV, which was filled with rowdy teenagers. Another one of those moments on the Journey where my mind was saying, "Hey crazy lady, run!" and my gut was saying, "You'll be just fine."

Mike Rosenfeld's story is a little different. Mike was one of only a few white boys in a Haitian gang in Miami. At fourteen, when he was in the gang, I imagine he was a scrawny kid. Years later, his short body was ripped with muscle from working out, his skin tan and his hair shaved short. He was classically handsome.

Dafna with Mike Rosenfeld and kids

While running with his gang one evening, he was picked up by the police. His parents were given the option of letting him go to jail, or shipping him off to a reform school. They chose the latter. Mike spent his days in defiance, then gratitude, then fear, and finally in self-reflection. His life had been saved and he knew it. He felt he had to return to the streets and save the lives of other kids going down the same path on which he had been headed.

Mike opened shop in a corner retail space in the middle of gang territory. One by one, he brought kids into his space. He gave them access to learning about computers and about the music business. He trained them to advocate for healthy sex. He showed the kids that there were indeed other options for them. He modeled how they could make different choices, showed them that they did not have to die on the street. One night, as two gang members stood in the middle of his street pointing guns at one another, Mike stood between the cocked pistols and talked them down. No one died that night.

Todd Vinson was a tall man with rugged skin and sandy hair from time spent out on the ranch. He had an easygoing smile and bright eyes, and while he did not have a troubled youth, he was distressed at the idea that people could succeed or fail simply based on the families they were born into.

One day, Todd's uncle announced to the family that he was going to give away his ranch to whoever had the best use for it. Todd did not miss a beat in telling his uncle that he would build homes for boys who needed to escape violent homes and be nurtured through school. He won the ranch!

Todd built the homes, and he built a campground. He nurtured the boys and they succeeded, achieving the holy grail: college admissions. After that, they did not want to leave. Todd could not kick the boys out, so he began sheltering them through college.

These three are men— tough men. When you listen to them, you know that their love knows no limits. They each received gifts—survival, rescue, faith—and they used these gifts

Dafna with Todd Vinson

to strengthen our society by lifting up the kids that the rest of society fears. These men, and the others out there like them, deserve our highest respect and admiration. They change destinies. They change lives. They are the people my middle school audience member needs to meet.

Chapter 12
And, I found my love

This seems like a good time to fully introduce you to my Michael. Until now I've only given you little peeks into him. I don't know if I could ever really do justice to who he is and what he has given to me.

Michael's eyes were sparkling and there was the tiniest hint of a smirk in his expression as he listened to me rattling off my latest grand tale. I could tell how truly thrilled he was for me with each new experience, and he listened patiently and intently as I regaled him with my adventures. As the year went on, Michael had to assume more and more of the maintenance duties of the Journey, not to mention bearing the brunt of the financial burden of my day-to-day needs, like food. I sometimes worried that sharing my adventures and excitement was unfair. I almost wanted to tone them down. Yet with each new state and each new adventure, he told me how proud he was of me. And he took care of me when I was too exhausted to move on the day each week when I returned from my latest stop on the Journey.

By the time I returned home from Ohio, my third state, it was clear that I could not continue editing the videos while blogging, scheduling the next state, and handling all the travel arrangements. It was just too much. Michael told me he would take over that task. While I loved Michael dearly, I didn't know if I could trust him to tell the story. He would have to edit the interviews down from up to two hours of raw footage to a seven-to-ten-minute piece for the website. The editor tells the story. Would the story he pulled from the footage be the same as the story I wanted to tell? I did not dare to disrespect him by telling him how worried I was. The following Sunday, I walked into his bedroom to find him sitting on the bed with his computer open in front of him, tears streaming down his face.

I ran over to him. "What's wrong, baby?" He just pointed to the computer screen. He was editing a video and was moved to tears. I knew, right then, that he would do just fine. Yes, the story he shared might differ from what I might have chosen, but it was clearly going to be told from a place of caring and respect. And, yes, I fell in love with him all over again at that moment.

Throughout the Journey, Michael was my cheerleader, my web designer, my video editor, my co-parent, my best friend, and my lover. He was the rock that I leaned on when I was tired, when I was sick, and when I was homesick. He shared each trip with me through the videos he edited, and he, too, fell in love with the people of America.

Michael and I first laid eyes on each other at the Starbucks conveniently situated between our offices. I was working at a hospital, and he was at our NBC affiliate. The morning line was notoriously long, and as we stood there, he asked me about the cast on my wrist. He loves to tell this story, and I always love hearing him tell it.

I told him the story of how I had kicked my own wrist doing Tae Bo . . . by myself. He was amused by the thought that someone could actually do that. I even demonstrated the move in slow motion for him.

I very clearly remember telling him I was certain we had met before. He wasn't an avid coffee drinker—at this point he maybe had a Frappuccino a year—so it was not simply a matter of having seen him in the shop before. We never found any mutual connections. I just remember looking into those soulful eyes and knowing, without a doubt, that I had lost myself in the depths of them before.

In this country, girls are raised (at least I was) to look for fairy tales. Look for the man who will sweep you off your feet and protect you. None of our fairy tales talked about hard work, unpacking each other's proverbial baggage, or handling illness, death, and children. The fairy tales didn't teach us about handling economic hardship, and never once did they teach us how to support each other's dreams. I had never seen this fairy tale play out in my life, and yet, somehow, like the masses of young girls before me, I was certain that I'd have my fairy tale. I simply hadn't seen yet whether the fairy tale would pan out for me.

There has been so much talk in this country about investing in girls, teaching girls, and working internationally to educate girls. I, for one, am a huge supporter of initiatives focused on girls. Much of my work today is focused on helping female entrepreneurs. I believe in women.

In Fort Collins, Colorado, I met Kari Grady Grossman, a feisty, driven woman with blond curly hair and a no-nonsense expression. Together with her husband, Kari founded Sustainable Schools International after the couple adopted their son from Cambodia. The original school, which was exceptionally successful, has since grown into a national network of schools, exceeding all Cambodian expectations. Kari explained it to me best: "Yes, we need to invest in our girls, but if we don't invest in our boys and men too, who will these now educated and driven women marry? If they marry men who have not been educated, they will be relegated to a life of servitude as they would have been before their education, only now they will have the dissatisfaction of knowing, of truly knowing, that there is so much more they can do."

Her words changed the way I looked at relationships. Her words changed the way I think about international efforts to educate. Her words reminded me that it is not simply that we need more female voices; what we truly need is balance. To elevate the whole of humanity, not just one half.

My own life is part of this story. Before I had synergy in my relationship, I could not grow and do the work I was intended to do, nor could my partner. When I found a partner who brought me the love and passion I needed, while also matching me in drive and determination, it set the stage for us to support and encourage one another, to reach for our dreams and build the life we wished to live.

The connection I felt to him gave Michael a certain amount of power over me, and, had he been a different person, our story would have ended much sooner. Michael is the big unsung hero behind the Journey.

A dedicated man to the core, Michael never does anything halfway. He was born in Belgium to a Belgian man and an English woman. The Jenet family made their way to America when Michael was just seven and a half years old, in search of a healthier climate and better doctors for his ailing mother.

Growing up in West Virginia and Indiana, Michael learned to work in the fields. He and his brother worked their way through high school to support their mother after divorce left the family facing hard times. Michael followed his older brother's lead and pre-enlisted in the US Air Force. He spent eight years serving our country. During those eight years, he rose through the ranks of the honor guard and, as is typical for him, gave everything he had to his work.

When I met Michael, he was working for Denver's NBC affiliate. His colleagues to this day speak wistfully of the days Michael was a part of their team. I had my first true insight into the man Michael was when I recruited him to volunteer for a gala I was working at. He was assigned as my "right hand man" to help protect my broken right wrist. He was told to show up at 7:00 a.m. on the day of the event. Michael worked next to me from seven that morning to two o'clock the following morning and never complained once. I had never met a man like Michael before.

It took many years before Michael and I were in the right place, both emotionally and personally, to have a relationship, but I knew when I met him he was different.

At our NBC affiliate, I would see him pulling late nights and even a few all-nighters to make sure the station was on the air. I always marveled at his dedication and work ethic. Perhaps it was unfair of me, but when the economy came crashing down and the daily work of the Journey relied on the two of us alone, I knew he'd be able to handle the job.

Being with Michael was also the first time I felt so fully cared for. With Michael, I could let my guard down, I could cry, and I knew he would hold me. I could get sick and know that he would care for me. I craved being taken care of. For so long, even before marriage, I was always the one taking care of everyone else's needs. I was ready for someone to take care of mine.

You know, it's funny when you reach that point of wanting to be taken care of. I actually felt guilty and weak. I once made Michael promise he would not tell anyone that there were times when I would sit on his lap and cry. Yet, as our relationship matured, I recognized it was OK to be held and cared for, and that he was still a man who needed that same caring for in return.

The Journey was definitely stressful for Michael. He worked full-time at a new job, leading a major software development project with an impossibly short deadline. At night, he was single-parenting his fifteen-year-old son through the nightmare of hormones and the early stages of adolescent maturity. After that, he was up all night editing the video of the Journey trip I had completed the week before. I could hear the exhaustion in his voice when we spoke. I was exhausted too.

My guilt would reach even higher levels when I returned home each week. I would be so tired from all the driving I had done that my first day home, it was all I could do to stay awake. Michael would tuck me into bed and handle the care and feeding of the family.

He believed in me. He believed in the Journey. He put everything in order and figured he could keep up the pace for a year. I worried about him. I certainly did not want him to burn out. I certainly did not want to lose our relationship over it.

This Journey was not easy. The personal, physical, and financial tolls were burdens I did not anticipate. I knew it was not going to be simple, but I truly believed that I'd be able to raise money and that as people learned about the work, they would be motivated to give. There were certainly several of my peers and other people I approached who contributed money, travel points, and places to stay. These people included Melissa Zales Koller and her husband, who generously made donations to the Journey, gave me a beautiful place to stay in Connecticut, and helped me arrange a full schedule of interviews around her state. Yet, even with the generosity of people like Melissa, there was simply not enough money to make this Journey succeed.

Dafna with Melissa Zales Koller and her husband

I believed deeply in my mission. I believed I was helping people see what is so amazing around them and within them. I believed I was accomplishing the mission of changing the mirror we use to reflect who we are as a society, providing a glimpse of good people to watch and read about. Through their example, Americans would know that that good also exists within each of them. All well and good when money is no object, but for me, it was a very real and very missing object.

I didn't have any money, and I did not feel comfortable asking for it due to the severe economic crisis we were all living through. Such hesitation is a big problem for a fundraiser. The economy was in shambles. I did not want to take money away from families around the country who needed it for their basic needs, especially since a vast number had suddenly found themselves without enough. I had joined the ranks of the uninsured and I was no longer able to meet my basic financial obligations, but I did not want to stop. I was scared.

On May 9, 2009, I sent the following draft email to Michael. Upon his approval, the email would be sent to our board of directors. I drafted it while my children played in the beautiful Colorado sunshine at the playground across from Michael's house. I remember the dryness in my throat and trying to hide the tears streaming down my face from my kids, who just wanted me to push them on the swings.

DRAFT—The Party's Over

Hi gang. It is with great sadness that I write today to tell you I have failed in my efforts to fundraise for the Journey, and have come to the point where I can no longer afford to pay for my mortgage and other expenses. I have used everything I have in the hopes and belief that this project would impact people's lives and bring people to action in their communities.

I know through this project, with Michael's support, we have told the stories of many incredible people in America. People who love their communities and the people around them, and have taken personal risks and financial loss to be able to help those around them. These people are our country. These people are the pioneers from long ago, returned to make sure our country once again realizes greatness for all who come here. I have been so honored to meet them and share their stories.

The burden of failure is a great one to bear, and it is upon me for lack of ability to raise the funds to make it happen. We have been so frugal, but there is only so far $18,000 can go. Had Michael not been paying for food for me and for my children, we would have run out long ago. I am so thankful for his love and support, and am so sorry for letting him and all of you down.

Now it comes down to my responsibility to shelter my children, and I am at risk of being unable to do so. I don't want this to end, but the grant process, which we are only now eligible to begin, will take too long. I hope I have made an impact. I hope people found inspiration in the stories we've shared. I hope I have made life better for at least one person.

I have plane tickets through the end of May and will finish those trips while seeking gainful employment. I appreciate any suggestions for job leads.

With heaviness in my heart,

Dafna

I hit the send button and felt a weight simultaneously lift off my shoulders and crush my heart. I believed Michael would be relieved. He was carrying the burden of my living expenses, including feeding and clothing my children. I knew he'd be relieved for me to be able to once again pull my own weight financially . . . assuming I could find a job.

Within thirty minutes, the light on my BlackBerry started blinking, and an email response popped into my inbox. I was afraid to read what he had said. I should have given him more credit.

His message was short and to the point:

Not yet, Loml. (We refer to each other as Loml—Love of my life.)
Have faith. Believe.
As the oft-used bumper sticker says, "Pray like it's up to God, Work like it's up to you."
There's life in the Journey yet.
I love you.

I packed the kids up from the park and headed to his house. As we entered, Michael was standing in the kitchen. I approached him with the weight of the world etched on my face. He took my face in both of his big strong hands. (To this day I love when he holds me like that.) His hazel eyes looked deeply into my own.

"We don't quit."

He said nothing else, and he kissed me on my forehead and pulled me in for a long embrace.

Michael held all the power in that hour, from when I sent the email to the moment he uttered the words that would ensure my success. He pulled me from the brink of failure. He stopped me from falling off the precipice. With those three words, he impacted all the people the Journey would reach in the following six months. He just as easily could have said, "I understand. I love you anyway." We would have moved on with our lives and I would have carried the burden of failure, in some form or other, for eternity. But that is not who Michael is. Michael is the embodiment of "We don't quit."

That night, after we finished the dishes and took the children home for bed, Michael and I sat down at my kitchen table and came up with a plan. Michael was going to liquidate his savings account. I also made a few calls to those who helped me at the beginning of the Journey and made a plea on Facebook for mileage points or other noncash assistance that anyone might be able to supply. With Michael's savings, and the help of our friends, we continued to piece the Journey together one small bit of help at a time.

Just shy of one month later, we would get the call from Oprah Radio that Maya Angelou wanted to interview me to share my story and the stories of several people I had interviewed. She was waiting there for me, just on the other side of the precipice.

Toward the end of the Journey, Michael and I traveled to Hawaii, which is thankfully part of America! Interestingly, while I managed to travel the rest of the country on my own physical might, the bags were simply too heavy to manage in Hawaii, so Michael had to accompany me. Way to take one for the team, Michael!

Dafna and Michael

In Hawaii, we met James Koshiba, a Hawaiian in his thirties with rich brown skin and silky black hair that framed his square face. After hanging out with a group of friends, he felt they could do a better job solving some of Hawaii's challenges than the state government was doing. He and his friends (about forty of them) joined together in a formal meeting and spent nine hours tackling Hawaii's challenges, only to realize that maybe the government was doing the best they could.

The group was not satisfied with stopping there. They knew that their core mission was to protect Hawaii, and they felt they could make an impact by focusing on sustainable living. They came up with the idea for a website where any resident of the Hawaiian Islands could post a sustainable choice they were making, like avoiding bottled water. Others could then join the posted initiative. At the time of our interview, over sixteen thousand had participated, and their impact has spread far beyond Hawaii.

The principle that formed the framework for their approach is *kuleana*. James explained, "Kuleana is the word we use to say that we are entitled to anything our hearts desire and we are obligated to create it." This word, this concept, encapsulated the way Michael and I aim to live our lives. That guiding principle of "responsibility to create because we are entitled to that which we desire" captured what made us such a powerful team.

The next day was my thirty-seventh birthday. Because I was born in November, it has not often been the case that I can dine ocean-side on my birthday. Michael sought out a lovely restaurant in Honolulu, and as we sat watching the glowing torches on the beach, he got down on one knee beside me and asked me to be his wife. In the background I could hear someone at the other table say, "Look, he's proposing!"

Everything stopped around me at that moment. I wanted to be his wife. I wanted nothing more than to spend the rest of our days together, seeking out our passions and building the life we both desired. I also knew that solidifying our relationship was going to be a major challenge for me with my family.

I put my face in my hands and I started to cry. Michael remained kneeling beside me while all I could think was "Here is this man whom I love so desperately, whom I want more than anything in the world to marry. I want to scream to all who will listen about our love, but if I do so, I lose my family in the process." You see, Michael is not Jewish, and I was raised from a young age with the knowledge that if I married outside of my faith, my parents would "sit shiva" (the ritual mourning practice) for me, and I would be dead to them.

My family, of course, knew about my relationship with Michael, and I'd had many heated and tear-filled arguments with my mother about him. I never really spoke about him to my siblings, and he certainly was not invited to any family functions. To marry him, however, crossed the line. I so desperately wanted to tell my sisters about him. He was such a wonderful addition to my life. Even some of my best friends recognized how good he was for me but said they could not condone it if I married him.

My connection with and love for Michael are otherworldly. I will never forget the afternoon when we were driving down the block and Michael's son said, "Hey Dad, we are studying about the Holocaust in school." I was getting ready to share all about my family's history, my own personal experience of study, and how I ultimately worked as a Holocaust educator when Michael replied, "Your great-grandfather died in a concentration camp."

My head snapped around in disbelief. This was my history. How was it that Michael's grandfather had perished at the hands of the Nazis? Michael recounted the story about his grandfather, who was a professor at the University of Brussels

Dafna and Michael

in Belgium. He was leading the student resistance. One of his students turned him in, and he was sent to Dachau and kept as a political prisoner. He was doing his daily exercise drills one morning when the man in front of him fell to the ground. Ignoring the orders of the SS to leave him on the ground, he was shot and killed on the spot as he reached down to aid his fallen comrade. He was murdered, as it turns out, three days before *my* grandfather's US Army unit came in and liberated the camp. Three days.

Our histories were entwined long before either of us was born. You can feel it in our love.

Michael had been on one knee for some time and was starting to get a little worried as he watched the tears streaking my face.

"So?"

"Yes. Yes of course I'll marry you."

He placed the ring on my finger and we embraced. In his embrace, I knew he understood what we were up against, and I knew that with him by my side, there was no challenge we could not tackle. It would not be easy, but there was no doubt in my heart or in my mind that he was my match in every way.

I cried the entire next morning, not knowing what to do next. I did not call my parents. I did not share with my siblings. I did not post it on Facebook or Twitter. I suffered in silent conflict with my gain and my loss.

During the Journey, I met couples who displayed the kind of love Michael and I share. One of my favorites was Joe and Nina Brown in Texas. From the moment I stepped onto their Houston estate, I knew I was in the presence of a couple with a deep, loving connection. Even now, I can recall the electric charge that seemed to flow readily between them.

Dafna with Joe and Nina Brown

Nina and Joe worked together in their family business. Joe said Nina had saved his life, twice, following two heart attacks. I was certain, after meeting Nina, that she simply would not let Joe go at any cost. When Nina's Parkinson's began to advance, Nina and Joe approached finding a cure and managing Nina's needs in the same way they did everything—together. They were not a couple who kept their work to themselves. They worked to share their findings, and their wealth, with others suffering and seeking a cure.

There were two things Nina told me that gave me a peek into their love and that let me know I was on the right track with my own love: First, she said Joe was her "right hand man." As you know, that's how my relationship with Michael began. Second, she told me that their desks were always five feet from each other.

When Nina told me this, I immediately envisioned an office with desks facing one another. What a dream that would be for me. After my Journey, I became a little (read majorly) obsessed with British royal history. We'll call it research. When I began learning about Queen Victoria, I learned she had Prince Albert's desk moved to face hers so they could continue their work and their love together (my interpretation). Today, I follow the same path as Nina and Joe, and Queen Victoria and Prince Albert—you will find my desk facing Michael's.

It took me a fair amount of time to write this book for you (more about that later), and in that time I have learned that Nina's prince lost his battle with cancer. She wrote of her love, "After a courageous fight, Joe passed away 10/10/12. He was my soulmate; he made me laugh. We were a team. And I miss him."

It was because of the Ninas and Joes that I met during the Journey that I knew Michael and I would make it. We would battle together. We would be each other's "right hand men." Our desks would touch as we worked, we would hold hands as we argued (true story), and our love would help us navigate any challenge placed before us. We were, and are, better together.

Chapter 13
I found sisterhood

I have two sisters. I love them dearly, but our relationships are complicated, and our lives are so very different that our bond is not what I would hope for. I always ached for sisterly love, and indeed, I have had a few "sisters by choice" in my life. On my Journey, I found sisterhood in a way I never expected.

On the sidelines of my first Journey interview was the photographer for the Delaware Sports League, Alessandra. She was a beautiful woman in her twenties with ash-blond hair that cascaded just past her shoulders and a smile that was full of life and joy. As I explained what I was

Dafna and Alessandra

doing, she told me about a woman who lived three hours south that I *had* to meet. I, of course, was thrilled about the introduction. You may recall that I departed for Delaware with no interviews scheduled. I said, "Why don't you come with me?" I really don't know what possessed me. When she said yes, I didn't know if I should be scared or excited.

I picked up Alessandra the next evening at her home. She got in the car, and we began chatting as if we had been sisters forever who had grown up in the same household. The bond was instant, and although we had six hours to spend together, I found I was sad when our time had to end. We connected on Facebook—thank G-d for Facebook—where we have managed to continue our friendship.

When I left Delaware, I couldn't imagine I'd have that great fortune again, but I did. These beginning days of the Journey were so challenging. No one had heard of me, and building trust was my number one task. That task, of course, followed that of figuring out how to travel every week with no money. One way I did that was to take people up on their offers of a couch or spare bed when I came through their town. Georgia was among the first handful of states I visited. A friend in Denver offered to introduce me to her cousin in Atlanta.

Dafna and Anna Foote

I showed up at Anna Foote's house at the crack of dawn after driving several hours from Savannah to meet her. Anna was an activist, raised by activists, and from a family of activists. Her cousin, my friend, was a state legislator in her thirties. I quickly learned her story and her family's history; they had been fighting for civil rights for close to a century. As she spoke, I saw a woman overflowing with warmth, who took me in, gave me rest, shared her passions, and then called me a sister.

It had only been a few weeks since I had met Alessandra—could I truly expect to keep finding more of these women throughout my travels?

And then in New Mexico, magic struck again.

Sitting in my own car, having driven to New Mexico from Denver to save money, I double- and triple-checked the address. I was in the right place. I was a few minutes early. My heart was pounding. I had been at this for five weeks, but I still got nervous and excited before I entered anyone's home. I had not prepared any questions in advance. That was not my style. I knew the questions I wanted to ask could only come following a connection when meeting face to face for the first time. I wanted to know the stories. I wanted to feel the emotions. I wanted to learn what it felt like to change the course of another's life—the very question I would be asked a few years later. I felt awkward as I gathered my gear, camera bag, tripod, and papers . . . and left my phone in the car.

I sat in Ronalda's living room, tripod between my legs, desperately trying to hold back my sobs to make sure the camera did not pick up the sound. My heart was breaking along with each blow to her spirit that Ronalda recounted. She grew up a Navajo teenager in New Mexico where "her type" was not welcomed. I had just met Ronalda a few minutes earlier. I showed up at her doorstep after a brief email communication, in which I had asked her to share her story with me as I traveled the country in search of community problem solvers.

When she opened her front door, Ronalda filled the space. Tall and broad, she had a warm bronze glow to her skin and a welcoming smile. Her thick jet-black hair framed her face. I never expected that I would meet a woman like Ronalda. I never expected to make such deep and instant connections. I never knew how uplifted I could be, all the while feeling every bit of pain that this woman, a stranger mere minutes ago but now my sister, had endured on her path. Now, she had become a voice for others so that they would not feel that same pain. I learned from Ronalda, and so many others along the Journey, that I had a lot to learn.

Dafna and Ronalda

Growing up Navajo was not a fun ride for Ronalda. Because she was a gifted student, her parents were often told that any effort to increase her education would be for naught, as she likely would be a jewelry seller when she grew up. This same ignorance followed her own children when their giftedness presented and she requested gifted testing. As she recognized the bigotry that was so vast in its scale, she began to train herself to be an advocate for children who need access to special learning opportunities. She gathered other Native American parents and challenged them: "We are born of warriors. If we do not now war for our children, what is left to war for?" Ronalda, an ordinary mom just trying to make a difference in the lives of her own children, has continued to fight for the education of many others.

I sat in front of Ronalda, collecting her story. I cried with her and I laughed with her. In a period of three hours, we formed a bond that lasts even to this day.

By the time I reached New Hampshire, I was on the lookout for sisterhood, and it still took me by surprise. In the state where the motto is "Live free, or die," it is not a question of whether you will participate in community problem solving. It is an expectation as integral as the freedom that everyone in the state clings to and lives by.

When I set out for New Hampshire, I figured that at the end of my first day of interviews I'd be able to find a Days Inn or other motel in which to rest my head. I'm a bit of a "pantser"—you know, a "fly by the seat of my pants" sort of girl. I had not had luck finding a hotel, and I just figured there had to be something.

As I made my way to the location of my interview for the day, I noticed a dearth of hotels of any sort. I was a little nervous. At the conclusion of my interview, the host asked where I was staying for the night, and I sheepishly admitted that I did not know. Without missing a beat, she offered me a bed in her home just up the road. This woman, Charlene, was dressed simply in utilitarian clothes, was about my height, and had dark hair, light skin, and a warm smile. She would become a very close friend.

It was not the first time I'd slept in the home of a stranger, and it certainly would not be the last. I was a little nervous, but I truly had this feeling all through-out the Journey that maybe G-d, maybe the Universe, perhaps a guardian angel, was looking out for me. I felt I was on a mission

Dafna and Charlene

for good. I was trying to make a positive impact in the lives of the people I met and the millions of others in America that I would never meet. I hoped this would keep me safe despite decisions that I ordinarily would not, of sound mind, make. (Oh, how I just opened myself up for my brothers to talk about my lack of sound mind . . .)

It was a good bet. Charlene became the Journey's top volunteer. She helped me schedule interviews in states like Massachusetts and Maine. Even during my visit to her home, she helped me secure interviews and a place to stay in Vermont. She traveled with me and we communicated regularly throughout the Journey. I'm referring to people like Charlene when I say, "Find yourself a cheerleader." She helped me understand that what I was doing meant something to others out there. She helped me understand that while I may feel crazy, I am not . . . entirely. I've visited her

Dafna and Charlene

Dafna and Charlene

several times since the Journey, and of the people I met, I find myself thinking of her most.

Each time I made these bonds, I wanted to stay forever in the towns where these women lived. How could I make such powerful friendships and just move on?

And then there is Kelly. Kelly is actually my sister—well, technically my sister-in-law. OK, to be more precise, Kelly is my ex-sister-in-law. Labels, thankfully, don't mean much to Kelly. Kelly has been in my life since I was sixteen years old. Any time I was within driving distance of Kelly during the Journey, which for her equals about five hours, she would join in my travels. This would save me the cost of a rental car and ensure that I would have a ridiculously good time, even outside the normal excitement of the interviews.

My love and respect for Kelly have always been high, and through the year of the Journey we grew even closer and more connected. She is everything I could ever have hoped for in a sister, and my children are so lucky to have her in their lives.

Whether my bond with them was forged through happenstance, connection, marriage, or other means, these women and the others I met along the Journey changed me and strengthened me through their beings. Alessandra taught me to trust and to seek lighthearted adventure as I launched this Journey. She had no idea how desperately I needed that lesson if I was to succeed.

Anna taught me that deep love and affection can be born in an instant, and can last beyond a first goodbye. Much later in the Journey, I drove from Alabama to Atlanta just to have the opportunity to feel that love in person once more.

Ronalda Tome taught me that we must reach deep within ourselves to find the strength to meet and carry out our dreams.

Charlene showed me that truly doing the work of the Journey meant allowing people to join my team in a way that was meaningful to them.

And Kelly showed me that sisterhood never breaks. Whether blood or water is between us, sisters find a way to unite and find the comfort, laughter, and support we all need to see the forest through the trees.

Without these women, and the many others who became my sisters over the year, this Journey surely would not have happened.

Chapter 14
I found America . . .
sometimes by accident

Throughout the Journey, technology, and the blossoming social media world, played a major role. I got the lesson of my life in New York. The week before I traveled there, I purchased my very first GPS device. I had been using the GPS on my BlackBerry, but it had no voice command. It was very hard to see and was dangerous to look at while driving. Michael and I decided that the investment would be worth it. I did my research on the best units, and then faced reality and bought the least expensive one that had decent reviews. My trip to New York would be the first time I'd be utilizing the tool by myself.

Upon landing in New York at JFK, I excitedly plugged "Niagara Falls" into my GPS. I settled in behind the wheel and followed every direction, turn by turn, that the lovely lady I soon began to call "Betty" chirped out from the device. I was driving for hours through some of the quaintest and most beautiful towns New York had to offer. Driving, and driving, and more driving. I kept thinking, "There must be a highway around here somewhere." I lived in New York as a child. I remembered trips to Rochester to visit family. I vaguely remembered utilizing some sort of highway system for those visits. Yet, I never hit a highway all the way to Niagara Falls. It took

Dafna at Niagra Falls

me ten hours from the time I landed at JFK. I got there with just a few minutes to snap a picture and breathe in the beauty. There was no time to see the falls from the Canadian side; even so, I was taken aback by the beauty, the spray, and the sounds.

That night I stayed with cousins in Rochester, New York. After sharing my day of interviews with them, I regaled them with the story of my drive to the falls. My cousin David, a contemporary of my mother's, was looking at me quizzically. "Ten hours?" he asked.

"Yes," I said, "I could not believe it. I feel like I saw every small town in New York!"

"Why didn't you take the NY State Thruway?"

"NY State Thruway?" I went into my room and looked at the settings on my GPS. Wouldn't you know it; it was set to forbid toll roads. It was the first of many escapades Betty took me on through the year, adventures that at times almost drove me off the middle of bridges and at times kept me looping in never-ending circles as she attempted to figure out where I was.

Dafna with her cousins

One day, when I was driving in Maine with my new "sister" Charlene in the car, we noticed Betty had been awfully silent. I looked at the screen, and the blue line was there, but no route was showing. We pulled over, took out a map, and discovered that, sure enough, we were way off track. My sister-in-law Kelly was always fond of telling me she was going to program Betty to scream, "Abort! Abort! Abort!" when I took a wrong turn. I was sorry at that moment that she had not yet gotten around to figuring out the programming on that.

On the way back to the correct road, thanks to our trusty map, we passed a Revolutionary War cemetery. As my Michael will tell you, I don't take my freedom lightly. I thank him for my freedom and for his service in the US Air Force every chance I get. I also thank my father for his service in the US Navy, and when he was alive, I thanked my grandfather for his service in the US Army. What an awesome experience it was for me to say thank you at the grave of one Commander Taylor, who was commissioned by George Washington in the Revolutionary War. We had discovered a sight, deep in the woods of Maine, that we would never have seen had Betty not let me wander off the route.

Michael's favorite Betty story happened toward the end of my Journey. To hear him tell it, I called him in the middle of the afternoon, and when he answered I screamed into the phone, "Betty's trying to kill me!" While I don't exactly remember it that way (. . . well, maybe I do), I remember being so frustrated.

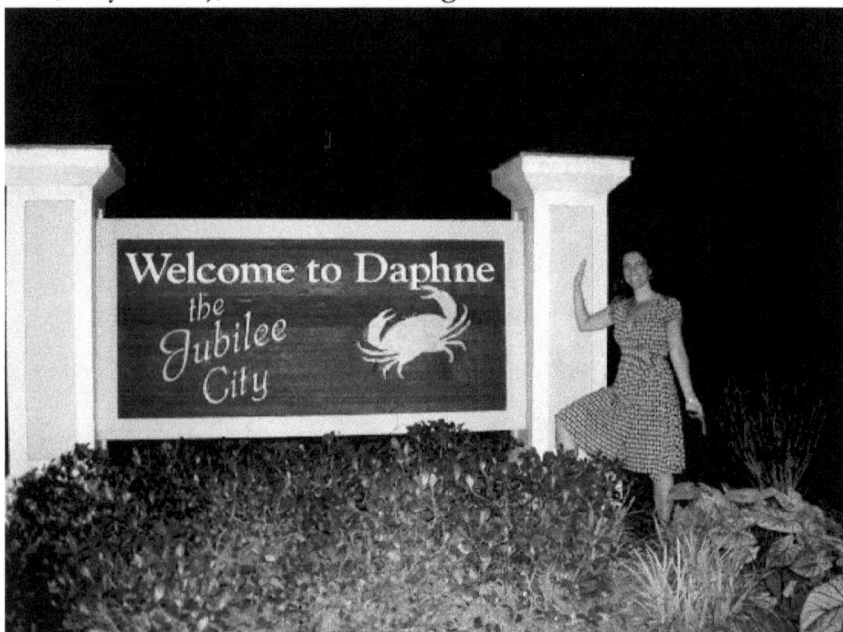

Dafna in Daphne AL

I was in Mobile, Alabama. I was heading toward Daphne, Alabama, and if I did not get going, I was going to be late. I had to cross a bridge to go toward the mainland. Each time I would drive across the bridge, Betty would tell me to turn right in the center of the bridge. There was no road there; I was in the middle of the water. There was likely *never* any road there. When I drove past the point in the bridge that she indicated, Betty would tell me to "make a U-turn now." If I kept going, she would navigate me right back around to the bridge. So you see, it was not Journey exhaustion setting in; Betty was definitely trying to kill me.

As the year went on, technology improved. With my switch from BlackBerry to iPhone, I gained access to Google Maps. This still did not prevent me from making some spectacular mistakes.

Did you know that in South Dakota there is a time-zone change in the middle of the state? I didn't either. Betty didn't bother telling me, if she even knew. Neither did Google Maps. This lack of information caused me to show up an hour late to an interview. This one, of course, had a journalist in attendance.

I walked in to conduct the interview in a lovely Methodist church. As I entered, the bell choir rehearsal was in full swing. Everyone was looking at me strangely. I was clueless until the woman I was to interview asked me if I was aware of the time-zone change I had driven through. I was mortified.

During the same trip, I was plotting out my travels and made an input error—a big one—as I was mapping on my computer. So big that it caused me to completely miss my interview on the Pine Ridge Reservation. I was in the far northeast corner of South Dakota, and the reservation was in the far southwest of the state. I was spending that evening in the home of the parents of a dear friend. My friend's father pulled out an atlas and strongly suggested I invest in one. Lesson learned. The atlas I purchased saved my rear in the several other states with dual time zones.

The atlas became a metaphor for the Journey. As technologically advanced and connected as we are, there is still no substitute for touching the ground, for shaking a hand, for hugging a new friend. This lowest-tech of solutions was a solid support. It never failed me. My atlas reminded me that while technology made my life easier, it was only one piece of the puzzle. I was often asked why I did not just Skype with people in each of the fifty states. They rationalized that I could still "meet" people and learn their stories. Yet, like an atlas in your hand, nothing will ever compare with a meeting that starts with a handshake and ends with a hug.

Chapter 15
I found stewards of the earth

I don't know that I ever really considered myself a "city girl" until I took this trip. I always felt that spending most of my childhood in Cincinnati, Ohio, made me a wholesome Midwesterner with a grasp on both the cosmopolitan and the mildly agricultural. No one need slap me in the face; my travels did that to me plenty. What I hadn't been exposed to was people fighting for the environment.

I arrived in Arkansas very late. I was supposed to arrive at my location around dinner time. It was already 8:00pm. I had been driving for hours and was still trying to navigate using the GPS on my BlackBerry. It was a darkness darker than any I had seen before, and the animal noises outside my tightly closed car windows were ones I did not recognize. My BlackBerry lost its signal; I was now trying to navigate based on what I remembered of the route. I was shaking the BlackBerry in my hand, willing it to come back to life. It worked! I called Barbara, my interviewee, and told her where I was, and she navigated me the rest of the way to her trailer.

An older woman with short, curly white hair and measured movement, Barbara welcomed me in and offered me food and a drink. I told her I just desperately needed to use her toilet. Barbara got a concerned look on her face and said, "It's awfully dark out there. I don't think you'll be able to navigate the outhouse, but you are welcome to use the compost closet." I stood there for a half a second and contemplated holding it in, but I really had to go.

I walked into the closet and peed into what amounted to a bucket filled with sawdust. I had all sorts of thoughts going through my head, but top of them all was what a crazy experience I was having. This would not be the last compost toilet of my Journey.

After I sanitized my hands, I came out of the closet. On the table was a bounty of Middle Eastern food. I had just told Michael that morning that I thought it was unlikely that any of the people I interviewed in Arkansas would be Jewish. Until this point, I had managed to interview someone Jewish in every state, and I was starting to worry that I was getting a skewed referral pool because of my network. I later disproved this concern, but not before finding out that Barbara Harmony was a Jewish woman who had moved out to Arkansas from New Jersey in the seventies. She had worked with Native Americans who were trying to save a healing well that had dried up. I couldn't believe it, and I couldn't wait to tell Michael.

Barbara Harmony

Barbara and the group she worked with did help bring the waters back. They started simply enough, by going door to door to the one thousand water customers of Eureka Springs. They found three hundred were willing to try using a compost toilet. This significantly improved the quality of the water, and afterward, Barbara continued to be a defender of water from pollution.

In both New Hampshire and Maine, I met with groups who were coming together from all walks of life to save their water. Charlene, the sister I picked up in New Hampshire, is part of a group called the PowerHouse 7.

Dafna and the PowerHouse 7

A large water-bottling company had worked some backdoor deals with the local government in Nottingham, New Hampshire. They began to build before the citizens got wind of what was going on. Dependent upon the quality of their well water, Charlene and her neighbors were not going to sit idly by and wait for a potential disaster. Neighbors came together, did their research, organized, and eventually put the water-bottling plant out of business before the wells were compromised.

When a similar situation began in Maine, Charlene and her crew advised another group of citizens who fought back. In each of the situations, the companies and local governments underestimated the lengths to which ordinary citizens would go to preserve the quality of their water.

Vermont truly elevated my learning about compost. I started my morning in Montpelier with the vibrant Buzz Ferver. At ten years of age, he became fascinated with the cycle of life through the ecosystems of the earth. He reached out to a man at the local science museum to ask him some questions. This man became his teacher and lifelong friend.

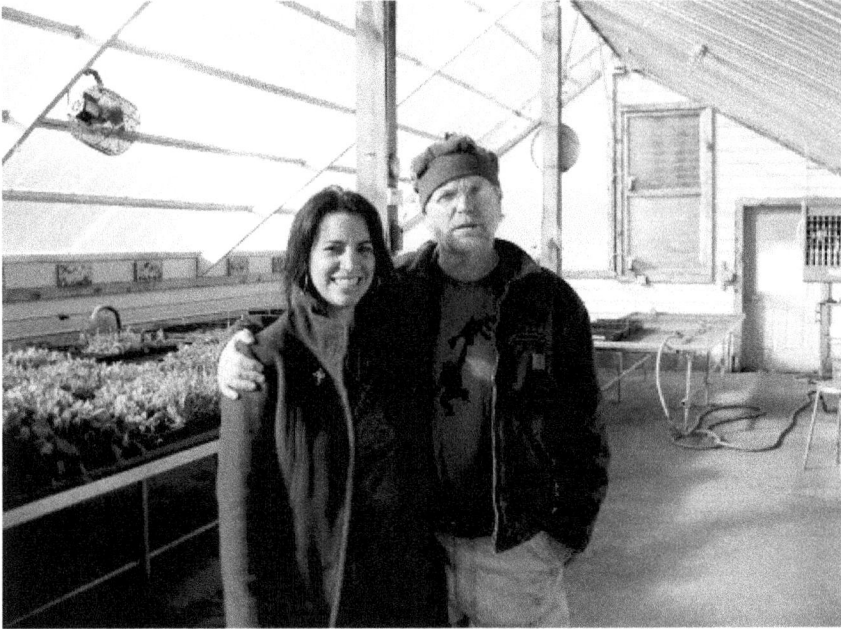

Dafna and Buzz Ferver

Buzz has spent his life learning about the land and the way it all works. He speaks eloquently about tying the pieces together to create a lifestyle of subsisting within the means of your local area. He works as much as possible to be a "locavore," eating mostly foods grown and harvested within fifty miles of his home. He lives on a plot of land, off the grid, with a high-level compost toilet and a living machine of plants that purifies his household water. It was truly amazing to see.

Self-educated, Buzz has read, and continues to research, all there is to read on his favorite topic, compost. He is a sought-after consultant to those interested in the hows and whys of composting.

Vermont looked to me like rolling hills of beauty, with winding lanes of homes

Compost toilet

and neighbors. The people I met there were connected to the earth. They were providing for their families from their land. They were composting their scraps and, well, their manure—all of it. So when a local science teacher, Tom Sabo, told me his students did not know where potatoes came from, I was floored.

When I laid eyes on Tom Sabo, I knew I was in trouble. He was gorgeous. Blond, blue eyed, young, fit—no, *really* fit (sorry Michael). All of a sudden, I was sitting in senior chemistry again where I had a teacher who looked like this. I would sit in class every day thinking about the Police song "Don't Stand So Close to Me." Yeah, Tom is that teacher, the one every girl goes home dreaming about.

Tom could not leave his answer at a simple explana-

Dafna and Tom Sabo

tion of the process of growing potatoes; instead, he planted a potato field with the students at the farthest end of the football field. Then, with reclaimed wood and the help of an engaged parent population, Tom and his class built a greenhouse. Today, all the food sold at the lunchroom salad bar is grown and harvested by the students. Tom did not have to take up this fight. It would have certainly been simpler for him to draw a picture or show a video. But, since he was connected to the land himself, he wanted to give his students the chance to build that passion and connection for themselves. The students eagerly participated, and so did the families.

The locavore movement, which advocates for consuming products grown or processed within fifty miles of your home, thrives in Vermont. Yet before Tom's project, the food served in the school likely traveled an average of 1,500 miles from farm to fork, as is the case for most of us. Tom's garden has literally brought that number down to 15 feet for his students.

A major goal of the Journey was to share stories to empower others. It had not occurred to me the lengths to which the sharing might go. A representative of the Milken Family Foundation saw the video I shot of Tom. He surprised Tom at school with the Milken Educator Award and a check for $25,000 to continue his amazing work.

Compost remained a theme for me, and while still in Vermont, I was invited to tour Karl Hammer's world-class compost farm. Karl looked like a farmer out of an old storybook. He was dressed in rugged farm clothes and wore a hat on top of steel-gray hair. A long, angular beard framed his face. His is the home of the Vermont Compost Company. Karl is one of the top, if not *the* top, composter in the United States. We walked around his farm and saw where scraps from the local restaurants were mixed with manure by chickens who had free rein over the property. It was an amazing operation to see.

Dafna and Karl Hammer

However, as his farm continued to grow in popularity for the high-quality potting soil and eggs it produces, Karl started coming under fire. His next-door neighbor wanted to put him out of business by proving that composting is not farming and that, therefore, he should not be permitted to operate under his small-farm license.

Karl believes that as the large farms begin to close and small organic farms begin to prosper, we will see a return to a time when people were interested in growing their own food and raising their own chickens to feed their families. He is right there, ready to teach us.

Karl wanted to give his interview at the top of one of his compost mountains. These piles of scraps were being processed by the chickens roaming everywhere. I looked up at the mountain and had a vision of what was to come, but I climbed it anyway. The video is pretty hilarious—so hilarious that Michael thought it would be funny to add the clip to the end of Karl's interview after the credits roll. There I am, using one hand to help me climb up and apologizing profusely to the chickens for interrupting their meal, and then it happens . . . face plant in the compost heap. You knew it was going to happen too, didn't you?

Dafna with the chickens at the compost mountain

I was so excited after my visit to Vermont that even though snow was falling when I returned to Denver, I dragged my kids to the local garden shop in a Colorado spring snowstorm. We picked up supplies to begin a small container garden on my front porch, where we planted carrots, garlic chives, broccoli, and cauliflower. My daughter, who loves to get dirty, was thrilled. My son, whose hands are always clean, not so much, but he did it. Each night until the weather turned warm enough to move the planters outside, the kids stared, watching for any sign of growth. I was ecstatic to finally have my first "garden." Perhaps it was something I ingested when I face-planted in the compost heap, but I certainly drank the Kool-Aid. Each year, my little city vegetable garden grew as more sections were added.

When I arrived in Boston to meet Jesse Banhazl, I was even more proud of our little railing garden. Jessie didn't believe that living in the city should mean sacrificing the ability to grow your own organic produce. Together with a partner, she founded Green City Growers. This company will come to your house or apartment and help you find the perfect spot for a small food-producing garden. Then they plant and help you maintain your garden to ensure that you can eat from your bounty.

Dafna and Jesse Banhazl

What I learned as I traveled throughout the country was that whether you live in an apartment or have a full working farm, there are choices you can make to connect to the earth and work the land. I had been surprised to learn that if I chose to do so, I could keep four chickens in my backyard in Denver. Those chickens would provide enough eggs to feed my family. No more emergency trips to the grocery store during a midnight baking binge! Karl taught me this.

Chickens may not be your choice, but perhaps a windowsill garden with your favorite herbs may be your way of connecting with the earth. Or, simply choosing to seek out local produce from a farm outside your city may be a good solution for you.

Farmers will share an alarming statistic with you. Two hundred years ago, 90 percent of Americans lived on farms and were producing food; today that number is between 1 and 2 percent. Some states are paying close attention to this trend. Norfolk, Nebraska, led an all-out campaign to encourage their young people to return to Norfolk after finishing college. They are investing in their next generation of farmers. They provide mentorship and money.

There are many ways to support the earth and make sure we have water to drink and food to eat. What role will you play in this story?

Chapter 16
I found ground zero of the economic crisis

When I tell people about the Journey, and the inauspicious timing, they are often surprised I was able to keep my commitment to avoid saying a single negative thing about the country. Just this week, my Uber driver was certain all the people I met on my Journey must have told me, "I can't help someone else when I've lost everything." That simply was not the case. Perhaps it was because I was seeking out problem solvers that I found stories of people coming together and helping one another. Or perhaps my findings truly are representative of the majority.

I am an eternal optimist. I have heard it said often that to be an entrepreneur, you have to be. I may take that to an entirely new level. When the economy began to tank in late 2008, I was fully convinced that we'd be back up and running at full steam by February 2009. Looking back, we know I was wrong, and as I traveled the country, I saw certain states were clearly impacted much harder than others.

The social problems that accompany economic problems are often those we'd prefer, as a society, to leave behind closed doors. Yet, people who managed to change their own futures also paid close attention to how they could help those around them. Las Vegas had staggering homeless and jobless rates during this time. Many ordinary people, living in community and doing their daily jobs, were looking for ways to retool how these problems were addressed. Others were seeking new ways to provide assistance, which ranged from helping with job placement, to helping people stay in their homes, to improving community safety at a time when tensions were at an all-time high.

Florence Rogers, a tall, no-nonsense English woman with straight, perfectly coiffed blond hair, was the general manager of Nevada Public Radio during this period of economic crisis. The station administration recognized that they were in a unique position to help their community, which had the highest unemployment rate in the country, as the economy slid. They altered their programming and began giving free airtime to organizations that offered assistance for individuals, from housing to job skill building. They used the resources they had to make a tangible difference in their community.

Dafna and Florence Rogers

In the part of Las Vegas that most visitors never see, I met Police Undersheriff Jett, a strong man with dark brown skin, a squarely set face, and silver hair framing his temples. Undersheriff Jett developed programs together with clergy and community members. Their goal was for the police or neighbors who monitored community security to know by name those suspected of carrying out crimes during this time of crisis. They hoped this intimacy would help people understand they had options other than crime, and that there were people who knew them and were willing to help.

A native of Las Vegas and a second-generation Las Vegas law enforcement officer, Undersheriff Jett and his team successfully engaged the community to reduce the crime rate by 13 percent. Through targeted community in-reach, the Las Vegas Metropolitan Police Department developed partnerships with clergy and community leaders to help them look gang members in the eye. Authorities responded on a "community member to gang member" level when violence and crime occurred. With the full support of the sheriff's office, these measures have not only reduced the crime rate, but have improved relationships with and acceptance of Las Vegas law enforcement officials in neighborhoods where they were once feared and mistrusted. In every sense, Undersheriff Jet and his team are purposely building transparency into their work, leading to a true community effort around law enforcement.

In Charlotte, Michigan, another hard-hit part of our country, Barbara Fulton, a middle-aged woman with short blond hair, had been working on opening a wellness center at the Hayes Green Beach Hospital complex. As her community's economic reality shifted, she realized that wellness practices needed to begin in the form of neighbor checking on neighbor. She wanted to make sure no one slipped through the cracks, that community members simply had enough to eat. Barbara is a native of this town of eight thousand and returned after twenty years of living in California.

A three-time cancer survivor, Barbara knows intimately how to help others going through major trauma. She is the Director of The Generosity Project. Grown out of what was intended to be a hospital project, it began when the hospital's leadership recognized the need for a town-wide project to truly meet the mission. Working together, hospital and town leadership toiled during this time of economic hardship to create a feeling of abundance and a tradition of generosity. As people mobilized, Barbara will tell you that while Michigan was definitely poor in cash, it was rich in human resources.

But what of the people, like my Uber driver, who lost everything, seemingly overnight, as the economy collapsed around us? In Los Angeles, I met a couple that experienced just that. Yaelle and Nouriel Cohen had a flourishing cosmetics business. Their success afforded them the opportunity to mingle with the elite of Southern California. When disaster struck, they found themselves going from wealthy to penniless in a heartbeat.

As you might imagine, Yaelle was distraught. She phoned her sister, looking for comfort. Yaelle did not quite get the response she was seeking. Without empathizing through tears or anger, her sister simply said, "Yaelle, if you are in need, you must first go out and help another." Yaelle took this to heart. She called a local organization that picked up leftover food from hotel events and delivered it to the needy, and she offered her services. From there, she began collecting clothing and shoes from community members and distributing them to others who, like her, could not afford them. As she and her husband helped others, they, too, received help. Slowly, they are lifting themselves up, and so many others are being lifted up with them.

During the economic crisis, the every day, ordinary citizen looked closely at their personal choices and at their places of work, knowing there must be ways to shift resources to save a population. Sometimes, being an intrapreneur—looking creatively within a company to bring about growth and change—is the way to create a sustainable answer to "How can I help?" And sometimes, being the one in need helps you figure out the best ways to help the others in need around you.

Chapter 17
I found the truth of our history

I'm embarrassed to say it. Before the Journey, I did not know the truth about America's history. Throughout my travels, I encountered the history and the current realities of the Native Americans in our midst. I learned of massacres. I learned of constitutions that predate the US Constitution, and which still govern many tribes. I learned of languages lost. I learned of forced conversions and humiliations. I learned of alcoholism as a stigma and as a problem. I learned of the inability of Indigenous people to get loans and to climb out of poverty. I never learned these lessons of American history in school.

I, who grew up a proud American. I, a member of a people who were also massacred and enslaved, and who often still find ourselves in tenuous situations because of our faith. I did not truly know of the acts of ignorance that led to the destruction, genocide, and forced relocation of the people native to our land.

Certainly, I learned of the "Indians" when being taught about Thanksgiving in early childhood education, but never did my classes delve into their history as I went through school. One may say that there is simply too much to cover. Yet, I feel that the time is now for us to understand the full breadth of our history. It is time to repent for our sins. Time to work with Native American communities, to heal the wounds, and to make an honest attempt at amends.

From New Mexico, to Oklahoma, to Maine, to Iowa, I met descendants of the Navajo, Cherokee, and Penobscot Nations, as well as others.

I learned from Jay Hannah, chair of the 2008 Constitution Revision Committee for the Cherokee Nation, about the Cherokee Constitution. I learned from former Senator Donna Loring, representing the Penobscot Nation, about the massacres of two tribes in Maine. I learned from Ronalda Tome, my new "sister" and a Navajo Indian, about the discrimination that members of the Navajo community still face in school. I also learned about programs developed by Native Americans. B-G Tall Bear, in Iowa, was adopted out of her tribal community. She now works to help Native American adopted

Dafna and B-G Tall Bear

children stay connected with their tribal heritage. And I learned about The Four Directions Development Corporation, which offers programs to provide loans for business growth and homeownership. The company was founded by Susan Hammond in Maine, a Native American who knew that providing access to economic stability was her way of helping her community. And I learned about programs to build schools and preserve language.

Dafna with Benny Shendo

During my first interview on an Indian reservation, I met with Benny Shendo. Benny sat behind his desk, his medium frame, dark skin, chiseled face, and dark hair representative of the features I'd grow accustomed to seeing in the Native American community. The interview felt awkward, a first for me. The whole time I was listening, my brain was spinning, asking me how I truly could know this little about my country and her people.

Benny is descended from a long line of tribal leaders, and when I met him, he held the position of lieutenant governor for the Pueblo of Jemez. Benny was the first Indigenous person appointed to a cabinet-level position in the New Mexico state government when he became the cabinet secretary for Native American concerns. Benny is proud of his children's success. He works hard within his community to ensure the continuation of the native tongue, Towa, spoken by only 3,500 people at the time of our interview. Benny spoke of tribal traditions, which are kept entirely secret to preserve the respect, honor, and culture of his people. However, he never once spoke about how we need to work better as a nation to build a bond with them.

As I reflect, I know I left there unsettled because Benny seemed to send the message that it's nice that I want to tell his story, but it's not really that important. He seemed to be happy to live and let live, and I just want so much more.

Although there are programs to keep culture alive, I learned that poverty and illness go unchecked in many Native American communities. Here, in this country, in America, today. Not in history, today. And I also learned about the struggle for recognition.

Donna Loring is a no-nonsense, middle-aged woman of average height, with short dark hair and strong brown eyes. Although soft-spoken, she wields power with every word. Donna is a descendant of the Penobscot Nation who grew up on Maine's Indian Island. When she was only ten years old, her mother died. She was raised by her grandfather, who was a constable on the island. Having grown up with the belief that the only way off the reservation was to join the military, Donna enlisted in the US Army and went to Vietnam. Upon her return, she followed in her grandfather's footsteps and became a law enforcement officer. Donna shared how her chief approached her to run for office in the Maine legislature. At first she declined, but later she acquiesced, "as long as I do not have to campaign." She did not campaign, but she did get elected for several terms. She only agreed because she hoped she could make an impact that would benefit her community.

Dafna with Sen. Donna Loring and Charlene

After conducting the formal interview about the impact Donna had made in her twelve years in office, I shared breakfast with her. She gave me some history about Native Americans in Maine and about two tribes that were completely wiped out, murdered, not a trace of them remains today. It became clear to me that the Native American story is not all that different from my ancestor's story of selection to be obliterated. The major difference is, my family's story has been taught in some schools for years. Donna's has not.

During Donna's tenure in office, she successfully passed legislation that required the history of Maine's Native Americans to be taught in school. This was a major victory. Donna explained her role as a warrior for the rights and the history of her people. As the legislation was signed into law, she stood in front of her colleagues, looked up to the heavens, and said, "This one's for you, Ma."

"Yet," she said to me, "until you and your people start demanding we tell the true story, the story will not be honestly and completely told."

This struck a deep chord in me. We know the story is not being told. We know that as a country building nationhood, we made many mistakes, terrible mistakes. Are we ready to stand up and own them? Learn from them? Apologize for them? Is it time we open the history books and fill in the missing pieces of the story? And can we heed Donna's call and ask for that story ourselves?

Native American communities are certainly working the country over, to strengthen their populations, retain their culture and heritage, and provide opportunities to their community members, but for healing to begin in earnest, we must all be part of that story. It was painful for me to hear. Was I supposed to turn around on my Journey and pick up the mantle here?

There were many times along the Journey that I wanted so badly to just put everything else aside and fight, but I had more stories to collect and share. And so, dear reader, I give this to you. How can we band together? How can we stand up and say we are ready to know the truth about our history? We cannot heal our bond with the Native American community until we honor them by acknowledging our history's horrific realities. Perhaps, if we start by teaching the history, we can take the next steps toward making amends.

Chapter 18
I found G-d

No, not in the way you are thinking. Nope, not you either. I learned on this Journey that G-d is a name people use when working on a mission of faith. I learned it does not matter whom you worship, or how you worship—when you are calling out the name of G-d as a reason for your service to others, you are doing good. Now, let's be clear: there are many who have used the rallying cry of faith to murder, defile, and force a belief system. That does not fall into my "doing good" category.

When I was invited to pray with people, as I was all over this country, I learned that the prayer of a person of faith was the most generous gift anyone could ever give me. And I learned that my own notions of G-d are not challenged when I bow my head in prayer and open my heart to the beliefs of another.

My first exposure to G-d was in Utah. I have friends who are Mormon. When I am with them, I pay attention and ask questions. I assumed I had a basic understanding of the Mormon faith when my Journey took me to Utah and I began interviewing members of the Mormon community. My first interview in the state was in the home of Kent and Joan Pulsipher—a lovely elderly couple. He was tall and she short, and both had heads of white hair.

Joan and Kent Pulsipher

They looked like they were made for one another. Kent and Joan shared their beautiful story of love and mission work, of devotion to family and ongoing service to community. I loved them instantly and could see myself as part of their clan.

As I was getting ready to leave for my next interview, Joan asked if I had ever been to a Mormon temple. I said I had not and accepted her invitation to visit a new one that evening, having no clue what I was in for. She said "Mormon temple"; I thought, "OK, I'm going to go see a church."

I had absolutely no idea.

My first hint of my cluelessness came when I casually mentioned to a gentleman I had interviewed that I was going to see the Sandy Temple. His response: "They're letting you in?" I was shocked; had he really said that? Was that an antisemitic remark? I just did not get it.

Dafna and Joan Pulsipher at the Sandy Temple

Upon arriving at the Sandy Temple, I began to learn. I did not know that only those invited were permitted to worship there. Not even all Mormons worship in that environment. I also did not know that the temple was modeled after my temple, the Jewish Temple, which was destroyed in 70 CE—the grounds of which are the single holiest place on earth for the Jewish people. I had spent three weeks praying and learning at the Temple Mount only one month earlier.

As I joined the VIP tour of the facility, which I learned is something that happens before the dedication of every new Mormon temple, I was amazed at the components I was familiar with from my own faith. The ritual bath, the prayer and study rooms, the style of devotion, all were modeled after biblical Jewish Temple days. And yes, there were many things that were very different from the Jewish Temple. The connection and spirituality in the space were overwhelming to me.

And then we reached the Celestial Room. I was overcome by the beauty of the space. I am sure that G-d was in that room. Tears began to stream from my eyes. I surely could not explain it to you, and no, I did not begin to want to convert, but I learned a whole new respect and an entirely new understanding of how this community celebrated their devotion.

The awe I felt around how people worshipped was also heightened in Chandler, Oklahoma. There, I visited the home of Todd Vinson, whom I told you about in the section on love. He impacted me in so many ways that I think he is worth mentioning again. His work is truly divine. Todd is the man who built a beautiful community of homes on his uncle's farm. He turned them into a place where young men in troubled and violent surroundings can find refuge and support to successfully make it through school. He has, in essence, adopted scores of boys and reared them through the toughest stages of their development.

When we had completed the tour of his grounds, he asked if we could pray together. In the past, I had always taken pause when asked that question, as I pray in a way that is very different from the way Todd prays. In Utah, nobody asked me to pray with them. I only thought for a millisecond, quickly coming to the understanding that the prayer he wanted to say together was a gift that could never be matched. I held his hand, and the hand of his best friend and business partner, and bowed my head in prayer. I listened closely, absorbing the meaning as he uttered each word: "In the name of the Father and the Son and the Holy Spirit . . ." I knew the words held different meanings to me, but it was the intention, the devotion, the connection, and the spirituality that carried his message. There was so much in each word that elevated me spiritually.

For most of my life, I have been surrounded by people of faith, so it did not surprise me that people of faith represented a large portion of the "ordinary everyday people solving problems in their communities." Many said, point blank, "G-d told me to do it." They said it almost sheepishly, assuming that I, as the listener, might recoil at those words or think them unstable in some way. But to me, those words meant that their soul was so connected to the Universe that when they asked a question, whether consciously or subconsciously, they could hear G-d's answer.

Elgin "Pops" Jones of Anchorage, Alaska, is a man who heard G-d's voice. An elderly black man, he is thin, bent over, and walks with a cane, but his physical image belies the spark inside. Pops heard G-d above the street noise of crying, hungry, poorly nourished children with "too much time on their hands and too little supervision." G-d said to him simply, "Feed the children and feed them well."

Pops understood that when the children were fed—if they were fed—they were eating junk. They received little to no protein and had no chance of eating a vegetable or some fresh produce. He went across the street to the community center and asked if he could use the kitchen there to prepare meals for the neighborhood children. Pops did not ask G-d why. He did wonder whether he had heard correctly, but he did not fear. He did not question. He prepared himself to serve.

Pops is not a wealthy man, but he found ways to get the food and the volunteers to cook and serve it. Mostly blind now, he can't see the details of the happy, well-fed children, but they still run in and hug him. They come in off the streets and get help with homework, love from Pops, and a meal to help them grow strong, healthy bodies. At the time of our interview, Pops's Kids' Kitchen had served over one million meals to the poorest children of Anchorage. Through his devotion to G-d and his commitment to his community, he figured out an answer to a question no one had asked him.

As fate would have it, a Jewish youth camping movement from "the lower forty-eight" was slated to volunteer the day of my visit. Knowing I was Jewish, Pops reached for my hands before I left. He took both my hands in his and said he wished to give me a blessing in my faith. He held me tight and said, "Shalom."

In those moments, faith felt fluid to me. It didn't matter the form of the blessing; it simply felt good. It wasn't always easy, though.

In Illinois, I had the opportunity to meet Manny Mill, a jovial man with white hair and a short, stocky build who had come to the United States as a Cuban refugee. He was an evangelist of his Christian faith. With Manny, I had to stretch beyond my comfort zone.

I found Manny through my kids. I had received a series of text messages from a parent at my children's school telling me about a group she had volunteered with when she lived in Wheaton, Illinois, called Meet You at the Gate. This organization picks people up when they are paroled from prison and brings them to a large, five-bedroom Midwestern home nestled in the heart of a small community.

When Manny, a rehabilitated ex-convict, decided to open his house to help others find rehabilitation, the members of the community were up in arms. There was no way they were going to allow ex-cons in the same neighborhood as their families, let alone on the same block. Manny persisted. He has a smile and a laugh that quickly puts people at ease. He and his wife worked with the neighbors and appeased them. They were willing to let him give it a try.

They named their house "Koinonia House" and applied to the prison system to become a rehabilitation site. Manny believed that through a significant commitment to faith and community, a parolee could learn how to return to society and become a contributing member. He himself had found a great connection to G-d while in prison, and he even traveled to Jerusalem after completing his parole. He wanted to give others like him that chance. Many groups already tried to help ex-convicts find G-d, but they were lacking the community connection element.

Dafna at Koinonia House

Manny pushed the envelope. He had convinced the community to allow him to designate his home as a rehab center, but could he also get them to welcome the new parolees? He went to his church and made a plea. He asked the congregation to help him welcome the parolees, so they knew they were a part of something bigger than themselves, bigger than getting through parole. For Manny's program to succeed, the parolees needed to see themselves as part of the community. His church community agreed.

Carlos, a parolee living in the home at the time of my visit, recounted the day of his release. Right there, at the gate of the prison, a member of the Koinonia House family greeted him. He was treated to a pancake breakfast, and when he arrived at the home, there was a party-like atmosphere. Members of Manny's church community stood on the front lawn holding signs that read "Welcome Carlos." He was stunned. In his entire life, Carlos had never had a greeting like this. For the first time in his life, he felt wanted and welcome. This was not what he had expected as a response from those on the outside. He broke down in tears.

Manny's work poses many challenges. Challenges he himself had to face in the process of rehabilitation. The challenges of moving the community to accept the people he was rehabilitating. The challenges of the rehabilitation process itself. The challenge of funding this work. Manny has had success, and he attributes it all to G-d.

Throughout the Journey, I was often faced with recognizing my own prejudices. Even in this section on finding G-d, I will admit that I sometimes found myself doubting. Manny prompted several discomforts for me. One is the discomfort of understanding what it means to be on parole. I had to face not knowing what the people I was going to meet were experiencing and thinking. Could I trust them? What about Manny? I tell myself that people deserve the chance to start over—but telling myself that and then having the experience to practice that thought are two very different things.

And then there was the G-d issue. Manny is an evangelical Christian. I am a Jewish woman. What would he think of me? Indeed, as I walked in, he made a comment about his G-d being a "Jewish carpenter." I knew he was making a joke to warm up the situation, but it certainly played to my doubts about his thoughts regarding my faith. I am a deeply spiritual woman, and I have a deep love of faith and the faithful, and still I struggled with the discomfort of statements made in jest that cut a little too close to home.

I asked to use the bathroom after Manny made his statement. I stood there looking in the mirror and questioning if I was the right person to be doing what I was doing on this Journey. Could I keep my mind open, remove any judgment, and allow this person in? I told myself that it did not matter what his beliefs were about G-d. Certainly they differed from my own, but so did the beliefs of so many I had interviewed.

As I emerged from the bathroom, Manny's warm nature put me immediately at ease. His strong conviction and faith were things I admired about him. They are indeed the things I admire so much when I see my siblings and the faithful families they are raising. The demons inside of me about my place in the world of the faithful were just that—mine. Mine to face. Mine to manage. Mine to release. Manny's joke was not the cause; it was simply my trigger.

What mattered most, and what mattered all the way through the Journey, was that here was a man who found a way to help himself, and who used his path to help so many others. That is simply all that matters in this world.

Chapter 19
I learned I have my own struggle with G-d

My own history of wrestling with G-d began when I was a young girl attending religious youth group programs for Orthodox Jewish children. Music is a big part of Jewish worship and I loved to sing. My father's Sabbath table was always filled with song and the festive giving of thanks, and I freely sang along. As I began to get older, I noticed that the teenage girls and women would not sing. I learned it was not permissible for men to hear a grown woman's voice in song—"grown" being twelve years and older. I was devastated. I asked rabbi after rabbi to explain this law to me, and as I neared twelve, my stepbrother began to leave the room when I sang along at my father's table.

By the age of fourteen, a series of events that happened to my family, and some to me, led me to decide that Orthodox practice was not right for me. I begged my mother to send me to public school. She finally gave in and let me enroll, much to the chagrin of our community. I stopped observing many of the laws of kosher dietary restrictions and began attending rehearsals and other school programs that took place on the Sabbath and other religious holidays. It pained my mother, but she let me be. It confused my father, but, as he lived half a country away, he did not weigh in on the situation.

Over the next twenty-two or so years, I fluctuated in my observance—from rigidly following the laws of dress, interaction with the opposite sex, and dietary law, to where I am today: spiritually connected but still struggling in angst with an unknown, and perhaps unnecessary, internal conflict regarding where I fit in the Jewish world.

For the most part, I had let this conflict rest unruffled inside of me in the years since. I told my rabbi that I felt we in Orthodoxy had gotten so far away from whatever it was that G-d had originally intended that we did not even know what it looked like anymore. I told him I'd return to practice when I was ready to sit down with the five books of the Torah, to study and determine what I think G-d intended in his messages to us. My rabbi expressed shock, and seemed to feel partially responsible for my departure. He did everything in his power to continue to make me feel welcome and respected in the community. Many others in the community simply turned away. If I was not going to live my life as they prescribed, then I, and my children, were not welcome in theirs. My family did not turn away from me; they just hoped and prayed that I would find my way back to the life they so cherish.

For the few years leading up to the Journey, I had settled into a routine and a comfort level with my life. I tended to ignore my inner conflict over my observance, with the pain only flaring up around Jewish holidays. But there are a lot of Jewish holidays. During my visit to Israel before I embarked on the Journey, I prayed mightily for answers to my inner conflict. I left the Western Wall on the Friday night of my thirty-sixth birthday, feeling a sense of inner peace and calm. Did I have answers? No. Yet somehow I felt a calm sense that I would figure it all out when the time was right.

As I told you, many across the country offered me prayers on my Journey. From the simple "G-d bless you" to the hand-holding cir-cle—eyes closed, heads bowed, ending the prayer with "in the name of the Father, the Son and the Holy Spirit, let us say, Amen." People of faith prayed for my safe Journey and carried me in their prayers.

At first, when I heard the path of a prayer going toward "the Father, the Son" . . . I became uncomfortable. That is not how I pray, and I had been taught that people in "forced conversion" situations throughout Jewish history would protect themselves by saying, "Da lifnei mi atoh omed," which translates to "Know before whom you stand." By declaring their dedication to G-d, and their Jewish faith, they were safe. Those words flashed in my brain, and then another thought came.

Certainly, I was not in any sort of forced anything. I had been offered a prayer and was grateful to receive it. What came to me was this: what gift could be greater to receive from a person of faith than prayer, their direct line to G-d? I cherished the prayers. I cherished them in the various phraseologies of different religions.

It was not until I was eight months through the Journey that a Jewish person offered me a prayer. I hadn't been missing it, or looking for it—not consciously, at least. Then Linda Greenberg, a slight and mighty sprite of a woman who has dedicated her life to serving the poor in Maryland and across the globe, offered me a prayer before I left her home. She grabbed my hands, closed her eyes, and began with "Baruch atoh Adonai . . .," which translates to "Blessed are you, Oh Lord our G-d"—the beginning of many Jewish prayers. I began to sob. Why had it taken eight months for a Jewish person to offer me, another Jewish person, a blessing or a prayer for a safe Journey?

Dafna and Linda Greenberg

I was filled with pain. All my insecurity surrounding my place in the community came flooding back. My feelings of alienation heightened. I wrote a blog entry begging the Jewish community to explain to me why. When my closest friend in Jerusalem read the piece, she told me I sounded angry. I told her I *was* angry. She said, "But Jews don't pray that way." We have a more formal prayer system; we pray in community, with a quorum, at prescribed times over prescribed things.

I understood where she was coming from. I softened my blog entry to be less of a rant and more of a request to the Jewish community that we consider sharing blessings with the people who enter our lives. I had been so touched by the prayers of others. I understood for the first time the power of sharing, even for a moment, in the faith of another.

A few years after the Journey, Michael and I were blessed with conceiving a baby boy. This child was so wanted and so loved. This child was never born. Five months into the pregnancy, his little heart stopped beating. I gave birth to a baby who had already left this earth. We were all traumatized and deep in grief. One month after I lost him, I had to travel to give a presentation in Seattle. I had been committed for quite a while to the engagement, and I did not want to let them down.

I arrived in Seattle shaky and depressed. So much was unresolved in my emotions. I did not blame G-d, but I needed some G-d to help me up. I sought out a Catholic church. Why? I'm not sure. Perhaps I was not ready to handle the flow of emotion that praying in a synagogue would have brought me. Because of the Journey, I knew I could go there and have my own conversation with G-d. The trappings and surroundings may be different from those in my faith, but the access to connecting with G-d was the same.

My own religious questions remain unanswered. That journey will be a lifetime journey. There is so much more there that I must discover and uncover, and I hope my own contribution to the world will be one where I help people to honor, respect, and even feel the faith of another, even for a moment. Can we learn to speak the same language? Can we, as a society, grow to respect the beauty in the diversity of faith in our communities?

Chapter 20
I found the answer to the question "What's in it for me?"

Women of my generation, and the generations that came before, were often raised to be nurturers, myself included. I was raised with the basic assumption that I would marry, have children, take care of them and my spouse, and contribute to the community while holding down a job. This was modeled for me and expected of me. In the process of rearing children this way, we often teach them that "What's in it for me?" is the most selfish part of any decision. We teach that we must think about the "other" before ourselves. What if we have been going about this all wrong?

During the Journey, Jan West, daughter of Dan West, shared the story of her late father. Dan was a man who lived a simple and fulfilling life as an Indiana farmer, but his heartstrings were tugged by the stories of those suffering in the wake of life after war. He traveled on a mission across the globe and was given the task of doling out infant formula. At one point, the formula rations were getting very low, and Dan was told to start figuring out

Dafna and Jan West

which babies had the greatest likelihood of thriving. Only those babies were to be given formula. The rest would be left to die.

To Dan, a farmer, this was ridiculous. He knew that if he could get his hands on a cow, all the babies could get fed. He reached out to his fellow farmers in Indiana and explained the choice he had been told to make. With their help, three cows named Faith, Hope, and Glory were secured and then shipped across the globe to help the babies and their families.

This was not Dan's community. These were not "his people." There was not a thought of "yours," "mine," and "ours." Dan simply looked at the world as one family in which we are all responsible for the well-being of the other. He faced a problem, and without asking for permission, he went out and found a solution. His solution is still in action today. It has grown into an organization called Heifer International, with 650 employees working to secure the peaceful growth and sustainability of communities. It is now his daughter who continues the work set into motion a generation before by her father, his friends, and Faith, Hope, and Glory.

I am certain that, in the moment, Dan did not set out to create an organization with the magnitude and reach of Heifer. It was not a master plan. He was simply a man faced with an excruciating decision. He was asked to play G-d and choose who should live and who should die. He was not willing to play that role. He felt everyone should have an equal chance to live.

By boiling down the lessons I learned from the people of America, I learned to look anew at the question, "What's in it for me?" Dan wanted every baby to live and to thrive. He needed to solve that problem, to be able to go home to America and continue his life as a husband, father, and farmer. He was stuck. To free himself of a potential lifetime of nightmares as he thought of the babies who may have died because he denied them formula, he instead figured out how to save them.

"What's in it for me?" It may not seem like it, but this is a question Dan had to answer before he could put his program, which has continued since his passing, into action. He could not be responsible for the death of a baby. Not in such a specific, identifiable manner. He had to get himself out of the situation. I am not suggesting that Dan had this thought process, but somewhere at his core, it was this nagging question that thrust him into the position that allowed him to discover a solution. Not a Band-Aid, not a temporary fix—a long-term solution for the community he so desired to help.

Dan believed he would not only feed infants but also sow the seeds for peace and, ultimately, freedom—a mission Heifer International still pursues today. How far we still are from global freedom today, and yet how much closer due to the work of people like Dan.

A lifetime and a world away in Daphne, Alabama, near the beautiful shores of this state, came the call that would shape a community. Cassandra Boykin, a large, powerful black woman with short hair and large, intense, wide-set brown eyes, was out when her cell phone rang. She answered, and the frantic voice on the other end began to recount a horrific scene.

Dafna and Cassandra Boykin

Outside the African Universal Church, three teenage boys, ages thirteen, fifteen, and eighteen, had unloaded their weapons into another teenage boy, age nineteen, killing him. Cassandra was devastated. That was her church. She knew all four boys like they were family. She knew she had to do something.

The next call Cassandra made was to her pastor. She told him she had to do something to make sure this never happened again.

There was nothing for kids around Daphne to do after school, and the talk of bad things going down during the post-school hours was getting out of control. The pastor agreed to support Cassandra and the development of a youth center.

The center began with a trial summer program to gauge interest. They had triple the enrollees they expected. The parents were relieved to have an affordable option—just a few dollars per day. The kids were fed two meals each day, and they were hungry. Many ate like they had never before seen food. The center added an "afternoon snack" before the kids left, consisting of foods like spaghetti and meatballs. Cassandra could not bear the thought of the kids going home and not eating again until they arrived back at the center in the morning.

Cassandra is no stranger to the poverty these kids were facing. When she was growing up, she spent her summers picking potatoes and cotton with her sisters so they could help their mother make ends meet. Even then, she cared greatly for everyone around her.

She was visiting another church some years ago when a man got up in front of the congregation and said, "I want to recognize and thank the Lord for that woman." He was pointing directly at Cassandra, and she had no idea who he was.

The man started to recount a story from his own childhood in poverty. He and all his siblings would get on the work truck each morning with Cassandra and her sister. They worked the same potato fields. At lunchtime, the kids would all take out whatever they had packed to eat, but he and his siblings had nothing at all. Every day, he and his brothers and sisters would take a few raw potatoes from their pick and eat them.

Cassandra watched this daily ritual and was so upset at what she saw that she went to the man who drove the truck and asked if he would drive them the few minutes to her house each day at lunchtime. She would quickly fry up some of the potatoes so the kids would at least have some cooked food in their bodies. The man agreed, and that's what they did each day that summer in the field.

Sitting in the church, Cassandra could not believe her ears. The man said the difference she made in their lives was so significant. She made them feel that there was someone who cared.

With the same compassion she'd had in her youth, Cassandra, who had a full-time job that narrowly covered her personal bills, continued to grow the youth center to a full-time operation staffed by community volunteers. Kids are cared for before school, during school, and after school. The kids are nourished, bathed when needed, loved, and given a place where they know they will be safe.

Running the center has been a long journey. Many hundreds of kids have passed through. While each month she wonders where she will get enough money to keep the center open and running, Cassandra's faith keeps her going.

When she was seventeen, Cassandra lost her mother. She was very close to her, and the loss was tragic, occurring at that juncture between childhood and adulthood. On her deathbed, Cassandra's mother encouraged her to go to college, telling her that if anybody could do it, she could.

Working odd jobs to get through it, Cassandra went to school and became the first in her family to graduate from college. Her mother's words were so significant. So much so that today, she knows it is not enough to feed these kids and help them with their homework. Cassandra also sits with them and tells them she believes in them. She tells them they can do it. She encourages them to, at the very least, finish high school—a major challenge when parents are telling their kids to just drop out and get a job.

If she could mother them all and love them all, there would be no child in Daphne or in all of Alabama who went without. But the children of the youth center have her, and all of Daphne is better off because of it.

Cassandra too had to answer that question of "What's in it for me?" She was driven, and has been driven since her youth, to create a safe and nurturing environment to live in. She did it for herself, and she did it for everyone around her.

In so many of the stories I heard—maybe even all of them when looked at closely—the "What's in it for me?" will rise to the surface. Still, I want to share one more. One more story that when I heard it, my child-self cried as I dreamed that this man could have been there when I needed him.

Robert Lilligren was vice president of the Minnesota City Council, a tall man with long brown hair in a ponytail, warm brown skin, and a soft frame. As he started to tell his story, I was filled with awe.

When Robert was in his twenties and working as a bartender, he wanted to buy a home. There was a government program at the time giving incentives to people with low incomes to move into economically troubled areas. He sought out a neighborhood and found a condo on Lake Street that he thought would be perfect for him.

As he tells it, he moved in—and soon after, so did crack cocaine. The neighborhood began to decline rapidly. On one particular day, as he watched two young girls cross through a group of grown men fighting over drugs to get to the school bus, he felt there must be something better than this.

Robert believed that everyone—the girls, the other neighborhood children, and he—deserved a nice safe place to live. Robert and his partner set about creating that nice place by simply picking up garbage they saw on the street and placing a flower planter at his front door. Each time the planter was stolen or vandalized, he'd replace it immediately. When it no longer disappeared or got vandalized, Robert began organizing neighborhood gatherings to start changing the culture and improving the safety of his new neighborhood. Much work has been done, and many lives impacted by Robert's investment in his neighborhood.

Through his Native American heritage and European roots, Robert has a diverse personal history of overcoming obstacles and takes his commitment to children and community very seriously.

While Robert was sharing the story of the young girls, I was moved and began to cry. He was tearing up as well, but my response was disproportionate. I listened as he spoke and remembered my own experience living in a tough, low-income apartment complex in Queens, New York, right after my parents divorced. In a flash, I remembered anew the stabbing, the fires, the firecrackers, and the time I was jumped by another young kid who wanted my wallet. And I remembered going to sleep each night listening to the sounds of firecrackers and violence outside my window. I lived in fear in New York every day.

No Robert existed in my community. No one was going to make it better. As soon as she could, my mother got us out of there. The impact that community left on me was profound, and truly, I had not thought of it until Robert told the story of the young girls walking to the bus. How badly my neighborhood could have used a Robert. How different my life and the lives of so many others may have been.

At times like these in my Journey, I was struck with pain. I had promised to write only about the positive for an entire year. I don't need to tell you what is going wrong in our world. It is at your fingertips in a moment of taps on your mobile device. I know the world is not 100 percent rosy. I just don't understand violence. I never will.

There is no G-d, no Universal message, no deity anywhere that asks for war, conflict, terror, and abuse. No child should fear for their safety when they walk outside; none among us should be enslaved or go hungry. Not in America, or across the globe. The only way we stop the cycle is one person at a time. One person looking deep within and asking the question, "How do I make my life better for me, and who else can I bring with me on this path?" Freedom is the ultimate "What's in it for me?" proposition. Freedom is up to each and every one of us, and it is within our reach to achieve.

What's your "What's in it for me?"

Chapter 21
I found Zen in my mishaps

As the year rolled on, I got into a groove. I could quickly navigate most airports and board the plane easily. I had packing down to an art form. The morning I left was never easy, per se. All through the year, Wednesday, my departure day, was my toughest day. The kids did not like to see my suitcase perched on the end of my bed. They held me tightly, and I knew the pain of missing them. I was also sad to miss another three days with Michael. I would kiss him goodbye at the airport and hold him as tightly as the kids held me. Yet, as I worked my way through the sea of travelers, my sadness dissipated and I began to get pumped for my next adventure.

Landing was also swift and easy. As soon as the seatbelt light turned off, I'd grab my small roller bag, depart the plane, and head straight to the car rental. Once I selected my car, I plugged in my first stop on Betty, my GPS, and off I went. Snags were few and far between, but when they arose, they were biggies!

I only got stuck once. Delays were rare. Southwest was my airline of choice, and nine times out of ten, I landed early. The one time I got stuck was on a Friday in Spokane, Washington. I am still not quite sure what happened, but the airline I was flying canceled all their outbound flights for "weather," though no other airline had canceled any flights. I tried to get rescheduled, but by the time I got to a person, they told me they could not get me home until Monday. Monday! It was my "on" weekend with my kids, and my ex was particularly upset with me that weekend, so he was "not going to be able to help out." His right, of course, but there I was in Spokane, Washington, too far away to rent a car and with no chance at a flight on another airline that day.

Thanks to good friends, my kids had a sleepover Friday night with one friend and spent the day Saturday with another. Six hundred dollars later, I was able to get a ticket on another airline that would get me home by Saturday evening to pick up my kids. That evening in Spokane, after getting my kids situated, I lay in my hotel room and wondered what on earth I was doing.

Other goof ups were far funnier looking back on them. My first day in Washington, DC, was one of those days. I was staying with a good friend from early on in my marriage. We had both since become parents and moved on in our lives. It was great fun to catch up with her and spend some time with her husband.

Knowing that I was relying on my GPS to guide me through the streets of DC, her husband decided to help me. With personal knowledge of navigating around DC-area traffic jams, he routed me to ensure swift travel on the best roads through that maze of a city. That morning, I packed my belongings, loaded my equipment in the car, and took the direction sheet from him. I hugged the kids, hugged the dog, kissed my friends, and loaded the trunk. As I slammed the lid of the trunk, I had one of those slow-motion sequences going on in my head. The velocity of my movement was in full swing, and I could not react quickly enough to the vision I had of the car keys lying next to the video camera inside the now closed and locked trunk of the closed and locked car.

I am naturally a pretty calm person. I had given myself an entire extra hour and a half, knowing I would deal with some pretty awful traffic. I walked back to the front door and knocked. My head hanging low, I admitted my folly. My girlfriend looked up the number of the locksmith down the street. Her husband marveled at my calm. I knew there was nothing I could do. Getting upset and uptight was not going to get my car open any faster. Yes, I was embarrassed. Yes, I was a nervous wreck. But I was stuck and just had to wait it out.

In no time, the locksmith came and popped open the front door, giving me access to the trunk release, and sent me on my merry way. I was relieved, and I was not going to be late. See, no need to worry.

I was off. I set out into the DC traffic and made it to my destination, including finding street parking directly across the street, with ten minutes to spare. I rang the buzzer and asked for the person I wanted to see. My heart stopped when she told me, "There is no one in this office by that name." I looked at the board, and sure enough, neither her name nor the organization's name appeared. What did appear was the name of the last person I was to interview that day. My friend's husband had mapped my route backward. Now I was panicked.

I plugged the address of my correct first destination into Betty. I was relieved that it was only a few blocks away. By now it was pouring outside. I had five minutes to get there, find parking, and get to her. Needless to say, that did not happen.

My entire DC day, while filled with interviews with some of the most passionate people I had met on the Journey, was a complete disaster. Keys locked in the trunk. Wrong directions. Parking ticket. Betty sending me to gas station after gas station that was closed or out of business. One interviewee decided she did not want to go on camera. When the day finally wound to an end, I met my sister-in-law, Kelly, in Georgetown. I was so tired. As I collapsed onto the pullout sofa bed in her hotel room, it collapsed underneath me.

Even as I wrote the blog entry that next morning, I could not believe the hilarity of having that many calamities all in one day.

You would think I would learn from such experiences and never again put my keys down in the trunk of the car . . . but no, no such luck. In Maine, with Charlene Andersen by my side, I loaded up our car after spending the night at the home of Donna Loring, the Penobscot Indian I told you about. My plan was to conduct the interview, thank Donna for her hospitality, and then head across the state for my next interview. Once again, in slow motion—this time with Charlene standing next to me—I slammed the trunk shut with the keys in my view. I was calm. I'd survived this before. I knew the routine.

With barely a bead of sweat on my brow, I called AAA and conducted the interview while awaiting their arrival. The AAA mechanic showed up, took one look at the car, and began shaking his head. This new model of rental car had an anti-theft feature; if you popped the front door open without the key, the trunk release would be disabled. He told me I would have to go to a dealership and have a new key made. With said new key, I could get into the trunk.

The dealership required permission from the rental company in Rhode Island. I had neglected to tell the rental company that I had taken the car out of state. And so the snowball began. There was no dealership anywhere in the vicinity of Donna's home. So poor Donna drove us several hours to the closest dealership. Charlene and I got a good giggle; the guys at the Hyundai dealership were in stitches when I told them this was not the first time I'd done this.

Dafna at the Hyundai dealership

From that point forward, Charlene became the keeper of the keys on the trips when I was lucky enough to have her company. It was experiences like those, with people like Charlene, that made the Journey memorable on a completely different level.

I'm happy to report that I have not locked my keys in the trunk since. I came close once, but it has been proven that I can be taught!

As my travels, and my mishaps, continued, I started using the hashtag #PPEW, which stands for "Practically Perfect in Every Way." I loved Mary Poppins as a little girl and thought it was "practically perfect" to rope her into my Journey. I still use the hashtag today. Feel free to borrow it as your own funny mishaps occur on your journey.

Here are some #PPEW highlights:

@dafna_m 28 May 2009 Time for a #50in52 #PPEW moment: no cell signal, couldn't figure out land line, did, left message while the cell "butt dialed" 3x. Perfect.

@dafna_m 1 Jul 2009 #50in52 . . . #PPEW I have graduated from locking my keys in the trunk to attempting to lock my fingers in there . . . without the rest of my hand.

@dafna_m 3 Jul 2009 #PPEW #50in52 Left my clothes in LA . . . I
guess I can say I've given LA the shirt off my back . . . oy!

@dafna_m 8 Jul 2009 #50in52 #PPEW Rental car remote did not
work. No biggie thought I until car alarm went off upon re-entry
while I'm talking to a reporter.

@dafna_m 16 Jul 2009 Having one of those #PPEW #50in52 days.
How do I find gas stations with E85? How do I drive 5.5 hours in
4? Ideas?

@dafna_m 20 Jul 2009 Apparently Betty (my GPS) can't see Alaska?!?!
#PPEW #50in52

@dafna_m 19 Aug 2009 Ok, seriously now, who travels as much as I
do and forgets to pack underwear!!!???!!! #PPEW

@dafna_m 24 Sep 2009 Betty the GPS had me doing laps around Gulf
Shores, AL then she wanted me to drive off the bridge . . . should
I take a hint? #PPEW

@dafna_m 15 Oct 2009 #50in52 #PPEW Headed back to Dawn, MO
to retrieve the battery I left. :-(

If this Journey has taught me anything at all, it is this: you can get
worked up and you can stress, or you can laugh and breathe. Choose
laughter. The result will be the same in the end. Oh, and if you can
laugh with others, it's even better!

Chapter 22
I found social media—and I love social media

Hashtags like #PPEW, as well as meaningful posts on social media platforms during my Journey, taught me a lot. There is power in correctly using social media tools. And just like the news media, you need to pick your outlets and your "reporters" wisely—otherwise you may as well just keep watching the news.

Social media was a totally new area for me. While I had been an early technology adopter from a young age, I had not gotten into and did not understand the social media arena. When Michael and I decided to do the Journey, I understood enough to realize that social media platforms would help me share information about the Journey and get people excited about serving their communities. My first step was to create a MySpace page . . . I look back now and realize how much the social media universe has changed since the few months before 2009.

I hated MySpace. I could not figure out how to find people, make friends, or share information. I was banging my head against a virtual brick wall. After three weeks of whining, I gave up on MySpace and decided I would give "the Facebook" a try.

Again, I complained all the way. Wasn't this an arena for college students? How was I going to see any real benefit from my involvement on Facebook? I started my blog at around the same time, and it really felt like I was posting uselessly into the ether. How on earth was anybody going to find me?

Another three weeks and lots of complaining later, I received a friend request from a guy I had a huge crush on in high school. All of a sudden, something clicked in my brain. This guy had been popular in high school and now worked in the tech arena. He had found all our high school friends and was well connected on Facebook. He found me, then they found me, and overnight, nationwide friendships were established. In a moment, I totally got the power of connectivity on Facebook. I started making my posts more exciting and relevant, and my number of friends began climbing steadily.

As Facebook became a second language for me, I began the Twitter learning curve. Twitter took me a little longer to master, but it was a great platform for authentic networking. It helped me meet people completely outside of my social circle with whom I could learn, engage, and grow.

It was not long before I realized that, for me, the major value of these social platforms was in helping me find people to interview all over the country. Each week, I would post where I was heading next on Facebook or Twitter. I'd ask my network to tell me about the people in their communities who were solving community problems or otherwise working to build community. Facebook would typically net the most results, but I will never forget the day that I got my first 140-character nomination through Twitter.

I traveled to Detroit to interview a man named Terry Bean, who was entrenched in this new social media realm. An average-height guy with brown hair and deep brown eyes filled with character, his dark skin revealed his Native American heritage. Terry was helping to bring people together in Detroit. He and I connected, and I found my way to his office.

Terry is a man who places so much value on connecting individuals to the resources they need that I sometimes wonder if he forgets about himself. Through Motor City Connect, Terry brought the online world offline. His belief is simple: if you forge a relationship online, the

Dafna and Terry Bean

next natural step is to take it offline. The connections he has helped to forge have led to jobs, the formation of new businesses, and relationships that will continue to elevate Detroit, and indeed, all of Michigan.

When Terry and I connected, it was the first time I'd interviewed someone whose community was located in this new realm, this social media universe, which, nineteen states into the Journey, I was still learning. I'll admit I felt a bit of skepticism, until I met him.

Terry's tweets were definitely engaging, but it took meeting him in person to truly recognize his power. Terry is a man full of smiles, energy, and passion for the difference he is making in people's lives throughout the Motor City.

He spoke about the first time people who have engaged online meet in person, and the awkwardness of a junior high dance that fills the room as first-time attendees arrive at one of his events. Terry reminds people to consider what they need and what they have to offer. Before long, the mood begins to lift, and laughter fills the room as attendees connect the person they are meeting with their screen name.

In a time of unprecedented difficulty for the people of Detroit, Terry believed in a strong future based on their talent and dedication. One of my favorite memories of Terry is when he looked at the camera, pointed his finger in a very "Uncle Sam wants you" sort of way, and said, "We could use some more leaders. How about you?" Typical Terry—he is always giving someone else the opportunity to elevate themselves.

When we finished the interview, Terry asked how many followers I had on Twitter. I had never been asked that question before. I was so embarrassed, not only to tell him I was up to a whopping two hundred, but worse, that I was proud of that number. He giggled and said, "I can help you solve that problem."

Terry began to tweet about the Journey. Indeed, I got a handful of new followers that night and my very first 140-character nomination: I "met" @dixiedynamite, the fabulous Dixie Gillaspie. She connected me in Chicago, connected me to the "Go Giver" network, connected me in the

Dafna and Dixie Gillaspie

way only Twitter can do. Her first tweet to me followed Terry's night of tweeting to help me grow my following:

@terrybean 24 May 2009 Know any gr8 leaders/prob solvers in chicagoland? @dafna_m wants them for #50in52

@DixieDynamite 24 May 2009 @terrybean do you know @nextvoice247 and @briantomkins? Gr8 resources for chi leaders/ prob solvers for @dafna_m's #50in52

Terry never stopped tweeting about the Journey. As the year went on, he began sending me 140-character nominations wherever I was going. He continued sharing the news and progress of the Journey with his larger-than-life network that spanned Michigan and the entire country, always modeling his core value: helping others connect with the resources they need.

Twitter not only connected me to people to interview, but it also helped me defray costs by finding people to host me during a visit. Initially, I did not plan to travel alone . . . but you remember, the economy. Being hosted was a huge savings. However, as a single woman traveling alone, it also made for some nerve-wracking first meetings and sleepless nights for Michael at home.

One such experience was the tweet from Alisha Whiteway, @AlishaTV—remember her? The woman working to help teen business owners get their stories out? I met her after this Twitter intro from Brian Tomkins, the subject of an interview in Chicago that resulted from the first tweet I received from Dixie. See how this works, folks?

Brian posted: "@BrianTomkins 2 Sep 2009 @HeatherO @AlishaTV Plz show @dafna_m some Southern Hospitality as she hits the Carolinas 9/9 on the #50in52 Journey." Alisha replied, inviting me to stay with her when I visited North Carolina.

I took her up on her invitation, but even as I headed to the airport to catch my flight, I had not received a tweet with her home address. As fate would have it, this was one of my few delayed flights. When I landed, a direct message with Alisha's address awaited me. Off I headed to the unknown.

No tragedy, no drama, perhaps a lot of nervous anticipation, definitely many adventures. People opened their homes and their hearts as they welcomed me in. I undoubtedly had a guardian angel following me around the country.

I also learned about the power of internet radio for building a platform and spreading a message through the story of the incomparable Cyrus Webb. Cyrus, a young black man, looked like he could have walked off the cover of *Young Investors* magazine. He started his journey through a long-lasting love of books.

In Mississippi, the final southern state I visited on my Journey, I had been warned that I would find poverty, violence, obesity, and ignorance. This warning came from those in Mississippi's neighboring states.

The day I posted the request for community problem solvers in Mississippi, I received an email from "Cyrus Webb, President, Conversations Book Club, Meridian, MS." Cyrus wanted to be certain I knew Mississippi was not merely a state of bad statistics but a place that breeds leaders and thinkers. I was surprised and pleased when I received the email.

The day I traveled to Mississippi was a treacherous weather day. I had to land in Louisiana and then drive to Mississippi. I was excited to do this so I could take a selfie at the Mississippi state line under the "Welcome to Mississippi" sign as I crossed the border. By this point in the Journey, I had achieved elite rental car status, and though there was never a Porsche Cayenne to rent, on this occasion I had selected a sturdy Jeep Cherokee.

The wind was whipping all around me, and I thought twice about my plan to pull over. Mississippi was the only US state I had never been to, and even though my Journey was not yet complete, this would mark a major milestone in my life. I was not about to let a little rain shower keep me from capturing that moment.

I pulled over safely, jumped out of the car, snapped the selfie, and rushed back to the shelter of the vehicle. I was soaked. It was the worst picture I'd ever

Dafna arrives in Mississippi

seen of myself. Unflattering is generous. I didn't care. I posted the moment, and with my heart full, I navigated the rest of the way to Pearl, Mississippi.

When I arrived at the library in Pearl, a young man who exuded the confidence of one who knows the world is his oyster greeted me warmly. We sat down in a small library study room. I went through the video introduction rigmarole. He said, "Hi, my name is Cyrus Webb," and began to share his story. Cyrus said he was a Mississippi native who grew up loving books in a family that did not understand him but did support him. He casually mentioned that he attempted to take his life three times before the age of twenty-one. Then he just kept talking.

Cyrus, age thirty-three at the time of our interview, talked freely about his past. He knew that by sharing his dark tale, he had the chance to help another. Growing up amid the demons inside his head, Cyrus would escape in his books. He explained

Dafna and Cyrus Webb

to his family that to him, reading a book was the same as watching TV. He saw stories. He also learned through books that he was not alone in his thoughts. At twenty, after his final suicide attempt, he figured if he had not died yet, perhaps he was not supposed to.

Knowing that books brought him comfort, Cyrus sought a book club to join. He quickly learned that there were no book clubs in Mississippi that welcomed men. Undeterred, he founded the first coed book club, Conversations. As Cyrus would soon discover, he was never satisfied with "ordinary." He wanted to make this more than your ordinary book club. He started reaching out to authors to see if they'd join the conversations, either in person or on the phone. To his surprise and amazement, many of them said yes. Before he knew it, Cyrus was playing host to book lovers, authors, and people who had never even considered reading a book but who were intrigued by the topics and eager to meet an author.

Conversations has grown, and there are now many chapters across the country. Among other things, Cyrus now has his own radio show that follows his book club's model. Through it, he reaches out to schoolchildren and adults alike. His goal is to highlight great role models from Mississippi and beyond for his listeners. Cyrus wants the people of the world to know that there is more to Mississippi than the violent breaking news that always flashes on their screens. He also encourages them to join his addiction: the addiction to books.

In our interview, Cyrus provided a litany of people who he believes are the gems of Mississippi—people like Oprah Winfrey. As I listened to him, I just kept thinking, "No Cyrus, *you* are the gem of Mississippi, and I for one am glad that books saved your life." I'm glad Cyrus found his platform on social media so he could spread powerful stories and bring others along for a daily dose of inspiration.

As we wrapped the interview, I hugged Cyrus tightly, and he said, "I'm really glad you made it, considering all the tornadoes on your route. I expected you'd have to cancel." Rain showers or tornadoes, I got my selfie, and I got to Pearl. Gulp.

I made a promise when I started this Journey. A promise I still work to keep today. I promised I would not write one negative thing about the people I met or the places I visited. I did not foresee that social media, at this point still in its adolescence, would mirror the behavior of a middle school student. Many times, as I would scroll through Facebook and Twitter, I'd see people bashing others in their posts. These platforms are easily used to tear people down. But, as easy as it is to do that, it is just as easy to use them to build people up.

Choosing to avoid negative commentary forced me to figure out how to build conversation in a positive but meaningful way. I developed a short set of rules for myself. I did not sit down and purposefully design these rules. I watched them form organically throughout the year. I learned what worked and what flopped. Much of my work in the years that followed this Journey has revolved around teaching others how to use these powerful social platforms.

Here are my social media rules:

1. Be Authentic.
    Putting on a "persona" for social media is sure to backfire. Someone who knows you will call you out. Or, you will meet a social media acquaintance in person, and they'll find that the social you and the real you are very different people. From that point forward, you will begin to lose friends and followers. It is OK to be the real you on social media, even if that does not appeal to everyone. The people who are drawn to the real you—those are the people you want to connect with anyway. Trust me on this one.

2. Be Positive.
    This does *not* mean you must be all sunshine and fairytales. It does mean your posts should all be well thought out and positive in nature. When writing about life's dark elements, like

Cyrus talking about suicide, end with suggestions, resources, or links for help. Give people a way to take action.

3. Plan to Meet Face to Face.

Make it your intention to meet face to face with every person you connect with on social media. Think about that for a minute. What would that mean for you? What would it mean for the way you interact with the content they share? What would it mean for the way you wish them a happy birthday? What would it mean for the way we help one another globally? I had the opportunity to help my friend in Pakistan learn Lamaze to help her through labor. There were no meds for pain in her village. No doula to guide her. I sent Facebook messages with links to videos. She moved from friend to sister status. I will travel to Pakistan to visit her. Mark my words.

4. Show Respect.

Communicate on Facebook, or any other platform, as if your mother (or anyone you respect above all others) is reading each and every word. Sometimes we forget that the writer, blogger, journalist, actor, politician, or fill-in-the-blank that we are bashing is a real live person. The imaginary veil of anonymity that some feel when they post causes them to lose any filter they may use when coming face to face with the object of their ire. Some may think they are getting around this with passive-aggressive posts or comments. There is no power in that. Don't do it. That's not to say you should never disagree with a peer or politician. You certainly should when circumstances call for it. A well-worded response, one you would give face to face, one that leaves doors open for dialogue—that's the way to do it.

5. Oh, and never ever *ever* post after you've had something to drink.

Off soapbox. Now let's use this tool to build up communities everywhere, and let's start with yours.

Chapter 23
I found the power of traditional media

Media was a seriously tough nut for me to crack. During the Journey, I was sending out press releases every week and had tried to engage some pro bono help from some Denver PR firms, but no one was biting. I really disliked that part of my weekly to-do list. I was much more interested in trying to find great people to meet with and stories to share.

I did start getting picked up by small newspapers and magazines as I crisscrossed the country. One South Dakota journalist wrote after my visit that my blog was "predictably nice." I commented on my blog the next day: "Of course my blog is nice. I'm traveling the country to show Americans what's nice and good and positive about our country. If you want to know what's wrong with America, all you have to do is turn on the news."

In the process of trying to get people with media audiences to pay attention to the Journey, I stumbled upon Oprah Winfrey's Angel Network website. From there, I noticed Dr. Maya Angelou's radio show on Oprah and Friends, which focused on America. On a whim, I filled out the form, sharing about the Journey and my passion for America with Dr. Angelou. Several months later, I received a call from Dr. Angelou's producers. They wanted to know more, and Dr. Angelou was interested in interviewing not only me, but also several of the people I had met along the way. I was almost halfway through the country at that point. I could not believe it; I was going to talk to Dr. Maya Angelou, and some of the incredible friends I had made across the country would benefit from the interview as well!

I was standing in my kitchen when it was time for the interview. It was where I had the best signal on my iPhone. I did not have a landline, and I was panicked that I'd drop the call. As I waited for my moment, I began to hear Dr. Angelou speak about this woman, this "kindred spirit" traveling the country. Kindred spirit? Had Dr. Maya Angelou just called me a kindred spirit?! I was floating.

The conversation was a blast. Dr. Maya Angelou believed in my Journey. Dr. Maya Angelou cared about the incredible people I had met. Dr. Maya Angelou validated my sacrifice, my struggle, and my belief in the American people. When it was over, I hung up and called my grandmother, overwhelmed with emotion. All I could say was, "Bubby, I just talked to Maya Angelou, Maya Angelou, Maya Angelou . . ." I must have said it seven or eight times.

Not until the middle of the Journey did I find a PR person willing to help me out for a seriously small amount of cash. Once she got into gear, the story of the Journey started to get out.

It was October when the *Denver Post* picked up the story. I was expecting it but did not know exactly what day the article would run. The morning of October 27, my former assistant, Amanda, called me at six thirty in the morning, screaming into the phone, "You're on the cover of the *Denver Post*!"

I was confused. "What section?" I asked her.

"The cover!" she repeated. "You are on the cover of the *Denver Post*!"

I loaded the kids in the car and went to the closest newspaper box. Sure enough, there was my picture, above the fold in the top bar of the *Denver Post*. My hands were shaking as I tried to figure out how to put the money in the machine and get the paper out. I did not have time to read the article, so my daughter took the paper and began to read. She kept saying, "Oh my G-d, Mommy, this is so cool!" and my son kept saying "Wow, wow, yay Mommy!" It was quite the ride. I did not know that as I was driving them to school, a CBS journalist who had moved to Denver was reading the article too, and by noon, I had received an email from a producer for CBS Sunday Morning. They wanted to do a piece about the Journey. I am sure I stopped breathing for a long period, even while my heart attempted to struggle free from my body, using my throat as its exit point.

In November, the Denver NBC affiliate aired our story. I was in St. Louis and had just met another "sister," the spectacular Dixie Gillaspie, lovingly known by her friends and social media followers as Dixie Dynamite. I had spent the day learning from Dixie about her coaching methods, which help people achieve their highest good through the authentic day-to-day of their lives. Dixie is a woman who had to save herself from a violent past. She emerged as a butterfly from a cocoon of darkness.

The day had been so uplifting, and I knew that the NBC piece was going to air. I was nervous; I had not seen a cut of the segment before it aired. I did not know how they were going to choose to portray me. By that point, I knew good and well that the editor gets to tell the story; it doesn't really matter what you actually said. I trusted Kyle Dyer, the interviewer. We had formed an amazing connection through the interview, and I hoped I would be able to add her to my list of sisters.

Dixie, like so many before her, had invited me to stay in her home. When we returned, after a full day of interviews, I hopped online to watch the piece. I sat feeling humiliation pulse through my body, as I always do when I see myself on screen, but it was good. No, it was amazing.

I scrolled down the page to the comments section, and here the humiliation began. The comments were horrible. I was getting slammed up and down. Comments like "Who does she think she is?" and "What kind of a mother is she?" and "Are her kids just running wild while she gallivants around the country?" I started to tear up. I did not know what to do. Then, amid the comments, I found people who knew me defending me. It was the most surreal experience, and every muscle in my body was throbbing with discomfort.

I wanted the media coverage. How else would I get these stories out? My mission was to share and show the amazing goodness and power of our community. Why did people hate me?

The next day I had an interview with Gil Wagner, and I relayed the story. Gil simply smiled and said, "Welcome to the world of publicity. I'm glad the first comments were negative—it means you struck a chord and people will pay attention and follow." I was confused, and a little taken aback. Negative was not what I was going for. But Gil was right. By the time I finished, and by the time the CBS Sunday Morning segment aired, the tides had turned. With a few notable exceptions, every email I received was positive—very, very positive.

It was during the final months of the Journey that CBS Sunday Morning followed me to Arizona. With cameras focused on me as I interviewed my nominee, and an amazingly seasoned Barry Petersen watching me in the background, I felt so insecure. And my mother was there. The crew was amazing, and the way they worked with me was so respectful. I was really excited to see what they were going to piece together.

We had been given an airdate, which I quickly shared with my social media followers, and it got canceled. We were given another airdate. I shared again. Canceled, again. I began to worry that the piece would never air. I found solace in the David McCullough Jr. quote, "Climb the mountain not to plant your flag, but to embrace the challenge, enjoy the air and behold the view. Climb it so you can see the world, not so the world can see you." I had seen my part of the world, and maybe it was not so important that the world see me.

Just after New Year's, it happened. The first Sunday in 2010, CBS Sunday Morning told the story of the Journey, and Michael and I found our lives were forever changed.

Through achieving traditional media success, I would no longer be the sound of one hand clapping. People were going to learn about the Journey. The people I featured would find an audience. Americans would be inspired by their example. With the help of the media, I felt I had in some way achieved my mission.

As I reflect, I wonder if my struggle to gain media attention was my own fault. I was not shy about sharing my mission. I was going to "change the mirror that we use that reflects who we are as a society." The mirror I so quickly wished to push away was the mirror of traditional media.

I contend, and still believe, that much of traditional media is built to incite. Incite fear. Incite anger. Incite rage. Incited audiences are tuned-in audiences. "Nice" news is, well, nice. Positive news has not earned the kinds of ratings media outlets need to keep advertisers happy and keep the news coming. It's a cycle.

Many of the journalists I met over the year had jumped ship from traditional outlets because of the toll that writing and sharing inciteful content had on them. Studies have been conducted, and the reports show that the audience for positive news is not there. I wanted to change that. I wanted to prove there was an audience. More importantly, I wanted to reach the people who needed to be told to flip that mirror. I wanted to prove that on the other side of fear and aggression are people fighting a different battle. These people are fighting the battle to make lives better. I wanted to show that this alternate reflection was the true news story. I wanted to show people like you that you have the tools to be that story.

In the end, it was traditional media that gave me a moment to be reflected in the mirror.

Chapter 24
Did I find myself?

I want to tell you that I found me. I mean, isn't that the goal of so many of these journey stories? Finding self? Well, that's still happening and unfolding. I did find out some things. I found out that I could be alone. I found out that I could trust my intuition. I found out that although my Journey may look crazy to others; it was mine, and I had to take it to be authentically me.

I found courage.

Before the collapse of the economy, I had developed a business plan for the Journey. Michael and I used this plan as a platform for fundraising and applying for the requisite business licenses. In this plan, two people would travel with me—a videographer and a ground logistics person. We had also created a website manager position, as well as an editor position for the video content. The economy had other ideas. Michael and I would have to muscle through if we were going to get this done.

My first interview was with Robert Downing, or Bobby D, as he is called by the community he built. Bobby D looked like a dark-haired frat boy. Tall, with a medium stature, he was handsome and wholesome-looking at the same time. Bobby D

Dafna and Robert Downing

founded the Delaware Sports League, which provides a place for the people of Delaware to meet outside the bar scene and gather to play fun childhood sports, like dodgeball.

After getting into my rental car (and realizing this was the first time I had ever rented a car on my own), I plugged the address Bobby sent me into the navigation system on my BlackBerry and made my way into Delaware.

It was rainy and dark when I got to the school. That little warning sound that women are built with started going off in my head. "You don't know who this guy is. This school looks vacant. I don't see any other cars. Do you know what you are doing?" My heart was pounding out of my chest. I parked the car and walked in. There were one or two people in the gym. They told me I was in the right place, so I waited for Bobby D.

Just a few minutes later, this big guy, grinning warmly from ear to ear, walked over and took my hand. He was so excited to meet me. Me? I was so excited and thankful to meet him! His reaction took me a bit by surprise. I mean, really, who was I? I was a woman who got on a plane that morning and visited *one* state. But the Journey I was about to take excited him, and he was proud to be my first interviewee.

Remember how I was worried I would not be able to figure out the equipment? So, here I was, with this happy guy sitting on the couch ready to share his story with me, and, you guessed it, I could not figure out how to work the tripod. Then when I got that going, I could not figure out how to connect the microphone. Once I got that figured out, I forgot to turn the microphone on . . . Yes, Michael had shown me how everything worked, but in my moment of nervousness, I could not remember a thing.

When I was finally able to pull myself together and get started, Bobby D began to talk. He talked about his father, his wife, and his challenges. He said that he did not think what he did (creating a community that now numbers in the thousands) was a big deal. Someone had suggested to him that people needed to socialize somewhere other than a bar and asked him about putting together some leagues, and he did it.

He looked me in the eyes. The camera was not there. We bonded and connected on a level that surprised me. In an instant, Bobby became my friend.

The idea that I was going to have to be the one operating the camera had really scared me. I had only used a video camera once before, and it was when I was running a trip for teens to visit the Nazi-built concentration camps in Poland. I recognized I had a natural aptitude for framing a scene and capturing the powerful moments. However, after the trip, I felt like I had missed the experience itself. Seeing the kids experience Poland through a viewfinder was not the same as being part of the moment. I did not want to spend a year going around the country, only to feel I had missed it. During that first experience with Bobby D, I set up the tripod and only glanced every once in a while at the camera to ensure he did not move out of the scene. Most of the time, my eyes were connected with his, and I felt every moment of the interaction.

"Man plans, G-d laughs." It's true. One peek at the original business plan for this Journey is enough to see that G-d, the Universe, whatever entity you may believe in, was laughing until they could no longer breathe. Or perhaps there was a larger plan for my Journey than I could see, and I just had to have the courage to carry it through?

I saw courage modeled by people like Ella Ochoa, a middle-aged woman with a soft body and a face that reflected a life of hard labor. Ella had a plan. Her plan was to continue her family's tradition of migrant work. A third-generation American, as well

Dafna and Ella Ochoa

as a many-generation migrant worker, she saw no other future for her life. It is not that she disliked her life, or cursed her lot. One thing she particularly enjoyed was traveling for work. She married a man who, like herself, enjoyed working outdoors, and they had children. (Here's where G-d starts to laugh.) Ella and her small family were content. As she and her husband worked, the kids played near the truck wherever it was parked. They were happy and healthy. As the children grew, they went to school, and, like their mother, they were gifted students.

The children of migrant workers (even today, Ella explained) get a limited education. They are often gathered in groups and taught in a school gym by whatever teacher has an open period.

When Ella was a student, the nuns in one of her transitional schooling experiences pushed her to get a GED. This was a new offering in America. She was scared, and at first she declined. But she summoned up the courage. She stepped onto a college campus for the first time in her life to take a test that she did not think would amount to much. She had never seen a Scantron test and did not understand how to fill in the bubbles. She was terrified. She only had limited schooling. She was certain she was wasting everyone's time. She was certain she would fail.

She passed.

Ella loved her life and continued her path to the adult life of a migrant worker. She was satisfied. But her children were not. They craved more, and they begged for a regular school, a regular home, and an opportunity to stop traveling. As a mother who would do anything for her children, Ella told their father, "Either we all go 'inside' and stop traveling, or the kids and I are leaving."

Ella's plans were turned on their head. She loved her children and completely altered her family's lifestyle for them. Ella acted as the liaison between the schools and the migrant families. In her new life situation, she quickly became the only person capable of leading the newly formed Nebraska Farmworkers Association to be a voice for migrant workers and ensure their rights were protected. This was simply not the path Ella had laid out for herself and her family.

Ella was needed for far more than she could have expected. By following the needs and pleas of her children, she not only helped them, but she has helped thousands of migrant workers with stories and histories just like hers.

Ella is a path follower. It was not easy, but she took a leap of faith. She found the courage to believe in herself. When she took the nuns up on their offer, when she told her husband their lives needed to change, when she accepted the challenge presented to her by the Nebraska Farmworkers Association, she followed a path that was forming in front of her.

It became very clear to me during this year that I, too, am a path follower. It is not the path of least resistance—quite the contrary. My path sometimes appears littered with weeds, but underneath the weeds, it is lined with gold. How often in our lives do we see the weeds and turn away? I have always felt a need to dig through the weeds.

I learned to trust in myself and become excited for my Journey from Bobby D. in Delaware. I learned to take the first step onto the path from Ella in Nebraska. I learned kuleana—"We are entitled to everything our hearts desire, and we are obligated to create that which we are entitled to"—from James Koshiba in Hawaii.

The people I met gave me my mandate as I continued to find myself on the path.

I often wonder how much different my Journey would have been had I been able to hire the three team members I had planned for. What if social media had exploded in 2008 instead of mid-2009? How many more people would have heard about my travels and nominated people for me to meet? My plans certainly did not go as I intended. Money, for example, never came, and by this point in the Journey, I was struggling, uninsured, stressed, and, not quite halfway through, scared that I would not complete my goal. America had not experienced the financial recovery I had hoped for, and the country just kept slipping.

The path of my Journey was certainly covered in dense weeds, but I could feel that gold just beneath my toes. Every day I led myself through the wilderness. This was my Journey.

Chapter 25
I found I had to face my demons, head on

When you think about your demons, where do they live? Are they part of a past that you no longer visit, or are they present in your daily experiences? I don't know that I realized how many demons I had, or how adept I was at keeping them hidden deep inside.

Journeying around the country brought me face to face with my demons. In some instances, I had the opportunity to squash them. In others, I was simply taken by surprise and had to fight them down. Many days were spent with this invisible internal struggle. I had no idea how much fear and insecurity I walked around with each day.

New York was a challenge for me on a personal level. It was here that I faced my childhood experiences with poverty. My mother was only thirty when she was trying to make a life for the four of us. It was scary. We were poor, and I constantly felt unsafe. My relationship with New York as a college student and then as a young bride was totally different, but the dark memories of life in Queens in the late seventies and early eighties have always stuck with me.

I fear being hungry. I don't remember ever actually feeling hungry while growing up, but I do remember my mother struggling to feed us. Now, this fear manifests itself in the form of overfeeding. It's not a typo—overfeeding, not overeating, though I am certainly guilty of that too. Let me explain.

While attending college in New York City, many of the students went home over the weekend to celebrate the Sabbath with their families. I generally stayed in the mostly empty dorm, and the cafeteria was closed. I had every form of "illegal" cooking equipment in my dorm room. I would head to the grocery store Friday mornings and buy food for myself and the handful of friends that remained with me in the dorm. I'd buy enough to feed a small army. Each week, I would panic that we would not have enough. I was afraid I'd be hungry. This did not change when I ran my own home. I'd make a mad run to the store to fill up my shelves before national holidays or impending storms, when shops might be closed.

It was also in New York that I met Brenda Mims. Brenda, a short black woman with light skin and hair pulled back to show her full face, struggled with homelessness while attempting to keep her children safe on the streets of Syracuse. She found her way to the soup kitchen at the Samaritan House. As she began to receive work training, Brenda asked if she could volunteer on the line in the soup kitchen. Each day she saw new opportunities for improvements, from the way each person coming through the line was greeted, to the way the food was placed on their plates. Brenda was not shy about making her suggestions. Eventually, the manager realized that the best thing he could do was hire Brenda to run the line.

Dafna and Brenda Mims at Samaritan House

Brenda did not dream of running a line in a soup kitchen, nor did she dream of helping other people who, like herself, found themselves struggling with homelessness. Brenda, like my mom, and like so many other parents out there, simply dreamed of a safe place where her children could grow up, get a good education, and have enough food in the cupboards. As Brenda began to find her stride, so did her children, and so did the people who came through the food line. Brenda recognized each man and woman by name and treated them with dignity. Soon, many of these men and women began finding their way to success off the streets, thanks to an ordinary woman named Brenda.

Brenda answered the question "What's in it for me?"—the question I contend may underlie every successful community venture. I ask you to think about what *you* need in life. What is missing from your community? How can you take action by helping to solve a challenge that directly impacts you? When you can answer those questions, like Brenda did, you can begin to change your life and your community— and I believe that's how we begin to change the world.

The trek to Ohio brought me face to face with another demon; dealing with my divorce. Ohio is where I went to high school. I regard Cincinnati as the place where I grew up. It was there that I met and fell in love with a brilliant man who made me laugh and made me think, often in the same breath. I fell in love with him and with his family. Both his sister and father joked that if he did not marry me, they would. His cousin was my best friend and a woman I looked up to as a sister. I knew and loved his grandparents. It made sense that I would fall for him as well. When I was sixteen years old, he taught me how to drive a stick shift so I could purchase his cousin's red VW Rabbit GTI. By the time I was thirty-six, he had been a part of my life for more than half of it. And even though I believed the divorce was the right choice for us, and for our children, I still feel pain at the loss of my connection with his family.

Living in Denver made it easy to avoid those feelings, as I am not on their turf. When in Cincinnati, it is another story. My mother and stepfather still lived there during my Journey, as did all of my ex's family. I still maintain a close relationship with his sister, Kelly—the sister who joined

Dafna and Kelly

me on much of this Journey—and I like to joke that the judge assigned Kelly to me in the divorce.

Ohio was our first Journey jaunt together. Kelly is a woman filled with her father's humor and her mother's thirst for knowledge. Spending time with her is always a recipe for laughter and education! While driving from Cleveland to Columbus to Cincinnati, we laughed, we blasted upbeat musicals and sang all the words, and we stopped at every quirky landmark Ohio had to offer. She stood quietly by my side as we interviewed Alfred, the Holocaust survivor, who has dedicated his remaining days to encouraging people to celebrate and value life through his sculptures. We also interviewed the lieutenant governor of Ohio. He shared his decision to leave the nonprofit world, where he felt he could make a deep impact, for the political world, where he felt he could more broadly impact the lives of many more Ohioans.

Kelly has taught me many valuable lessons. During the Journey, she taught me that being divorced from my spouse didn't mean divorcing myself from my children's family. There are simply not enough words to describe the love and support Kelly shows for her brother, for our children, and for me.

I did not interview Kelly on my Journey, but her story is as valuable as any of those I collected on my travels. This woman has dedicated her life to being present to all life has to offer. She has also dedicated her life to giving love freely. Kelly took care of her Memaw until the day Memaw died. She helped care for the children of her cousin, her friends, and her stepsiblings. She cares for my children, ready to fulfill their every dream on the summer adventures they take together. And, while she desperately loves and desires everything in the world for her baby brother, she has also been there for me.

What's in it for her? I'm not 100 percent certain. All I can surmise is that she lives for adventure, and my children and I give her that in spades!

Dafna and Kelly

Dafna and Kelly

I didn't know if Kelly would enjoy this Journey. But watching her experience my Ohio interviews, and the conversations we had following them, made the experience so much richer. Her knowledge, her passion, and her sense of humor helped lighten the load and brought depth to the stories I would share.

She also kept me safe. Kelly is always looking out for her niece and nephew, and that means looking out for me.

We slept in the homes of my cousins in Cleveland and my cousins in Columbus. When we hit Cincinnati, Kelly brought me to my mother's home, where I slept in the very bed where I had spent my teenage years talking for hours on the telephone.

Which brings me to my other demon: no matter my age, I am always a child when I am with my parents. I am desperate for their acceptance, and I know I am not living my life as I was raised to live it.

I love the home I grew up in in Cincinnati. It is a three-bedroom ranch, maybe 2,500 square feet, situated in the middle of a long curvy block of Midwestern homes. I remember the first time I set eyes on the house. I thought we had won the lottery. Really. My parents moved to Cincinnati while I was in Israel for the summer. My trip was a Bat Mitzvah gift that many members of my extended family had chipped in to give me. It was my first time back in the country since my family had left for America shortly after my birth.

I had taken off for Israel from Philadelphia. We lived there in a tiny, dilapidated row home with a postage-stamp yard. My room was in the basement. I was scared of the basement. I'm still scared of the basement.

When my parents picked me up from the airport—the Cincinnati airport, which is actually in Kentucky, a fact that amused me—and drove me to our new home, this incredible sense of security washed over me. These houses were bigger than anything I had ever seen. The yards were enormous, easily big enough for a barbecue or for my brothers to play baseball with their friends. Not only that, there were front *and* back yards. I'd never seen anything like it. I was sure our family's future had changed, and I liked it.

When we entered the house, I remember standing at the bay window (I'd never seen one before) and thanking G-d for bringing us through the darkness.

Walking into that room always brings back all the emotions of high school. While "being home" is a great place to be, it always amazes me how much pressure I feel when I walk through that front door.

Only one thing was clear to me when I entered my home: I wanted to make my parents proud. Desperately. I didn't want to fall short.

Throughout the Journey, I worked on getting publicity. The Journey's goal was to get people to jump on the website and hit the fan pages set up for each state. Our aim was to gather information about what people felt was great about their cities and get them to tell us about nominees we might have missed. The more people who knew about the Journey, the more people we could inspire into action. We also hoped to bring attention to the programs and projects of these everyday Americans so that they, too, might benefit from a donation or increased volunteerism for their efforts.

The NBC station in Cincinnati was the first to respond to the press releases I had sent out before visiting Ohio. The NBC team arranged to meet me at the Winton Woods Riding Center. There, I would interview Dee Anderson, the manager, a woman my mother had nominated through my website.

Dafna and Dee Anderson

I was very nervous, and being accompanied by my parents only added to my anxiety. I had also arranged to meet my high school friend Alex, who responded to my Facebook post announcing that my daughter was selling Girl Scout cookies. He met me at the interview site to hand off some cash for donating a box of cookies to the troops.

It was brutally cold outside and there was no sign of Dee. I had left my paperwork at home, so I did not have her cell number handy, and I was slightly worried that we had crossed wires on the timing. My parents were sitting quietly in the car with me, not saying a thing and letting me handle the worry part. They were great, but the truth is, I wished they had not been there at that moment.

When Dee finally arrived, we began the interview, and she showed me around the campus. A tall woman with short blond hair and a muscular build, Dee shared about her background with horses, and about how training children and adults with disabilities to ride and care for the animals had changed her life.

The value of animals in the lives of people with disabilities has been studied over and over again, and Dee knew all the benefits and could clearly state them. Yet, she made me turn off the camera when she began to cry while sharing the story of a rider friend. This friend had been paralyzed in a riding accident. Watching her get back up on the horse and ride again made Dee truly understand the strength of the human spirit and the bond that people and horses share.

My hands were frostbitten by the end of the interview, but my heart was filled with the stories of how many lives Dee was able to touch at Winton Woods. I packed up my equipment, feeling a little heartbroken that NBC never showed. I had to swallow the disappointment in front of my parents. I wanted—I needed—to be strong.

I know that my mother didn't care whether the news showed up to cover my story. I know she was proud of me. I also know that she was worried. She worried about my health. She worried about my finances. She worried about my children and my future. She worried about my faith. And, while she told me she was proud, my demons prevented me from hearing it.

And then there were the demons of my past, the history I did not live but my ancestors did. I had been so eager for my mom to engage in my Journey. She did not read my blog but instead wanted me to tell her about my experiences, and sometimes that was really hard for me. I was exhausted. I wanted to encourage her, so I made sure to specifically invite her to nominate people for me to interview. When I told her I was going to Tennessee, she had one word for me: "paperclips."

While chatting on the phone with her following my day of interviews in Nashville, my mother asked when I was going to see "the paperclips people." I laid my head on the table at Starbucks and thought, "Oh my G-d." My mother had nominated Linda Hooper and the Paper Clips Project in Whitwell, Tennessee, maybe five minutes after I launched my website back in late 2008, and I had forgotten to arrange an interview.

I hung up with her immediately, then researched the school on my iPhone and tried to reach someone, anyone. When the secretary answered, I explained who I was and asked if there would be any way I could see the exhibit, and would *anyone* be available to talk to me about what the project has meant to the community.

To my amazement, the secretary told me that Ms. Hooper, the principal, would be there and available to meet with me. I could not believe my luck. I hightailed it to my last interview in Nashville and then hit the road for Whitwell.

As I approached the town, I noticed several homes proudly displaying the Confederate flag. It was not the first time I'd seen this. Yet, every time I saw one, I made judgments. Judgments I had no right to make. These judgments led me to fear that I was deep in the heart of our nation's bigotry and ignorance, and as a Jewish woman traveling alone, I feared I was putting myself in harm's way.

I arrived after school hours, and the building was locked up tight. There in front of the school sat a Nazi boxcar surrounded by a gate and beautiful sculptures of butterflies. The address of the school: 1 Butterfly Lane. I walked around and marveled at this boxcar sitting in the most unexpected spot in America. This small town, not known for being the home of any Jewish residents, supported a children's Holocaust memorial. As I stood there in wonder, Ms. Hooper walked up to me.

After introductions, she walked me through the resource room at the front of the school, which was filled with Jewish artifacts. My mind just reeled at the sight: a Torah in a beautiful wooden case, silver Passover plates, candlesticks, and wine chalices—all the ritual objects one might find in a synagogue or a Jewish home lined the room.

We sat down in Ms. Hooper's office. She began to weave the story of how she had wanted to teach her students about the world around them. She wanted them to study different cultures; she wanted to show them how bullying was problematic. She talked with her colleagues about her challenge, and someone suggested she look into the study of the Holocaust. She had a moment of pause. Jewish people were all over the world, their culture old and historic, their lives much different, religiously and culturally, than the lives of those in Whitwell, Tennessee. For these reasons, and because of the persecution based on hatred and propaganda that Jewish people faced during the Holocaust, Ms. Hooper felt a Holocaust study would be the way to introduce her students to the world.

She talked to only one teacher, who eagerly began teaching a class about the Holocaust, on a voluntary basis, for students and their parents. The community ate it up. The students came to Ms. Hooper and asked if she could grasp the concept of six million Jewish Holocaust victims because they could not. Although she'd been to some of the largest cities in the world, Ms. Hooper could in no way visualize six million people.

The students were desperate to try to grasp the enormity of the number. They wanted to collect "something." Their directive from Ms. Hooper: as long as it has something to do with the Holocaust, the school would support the collection. As it happened, a Jewish man in Norway had invented the paperclip, and the Norwegians wore paperclips on their lapels to protest the genocide of the Holocaust. The students were given the go-ahead, and as word got out, the project became a phenomenon. Holocaust survivors and so many others around the *world* began sending paperclips, as well as letters and artifacts.

Twenty-four million paperclips later, Ms. Hooper had the "crazy" thought that she would like an authentic Holocaust-era Nazi boxcar to house them. Miracles happened. People she would have never met if not for her desire to teach her students about the world began moving mountains. As those mountains moved, an authentic Nazi boxcar made its way from Germany to Whitwell, Tennessee.

As Ms. Hooper shared her story with me, I marveled. I thought about my own family being persecuted by the Nazis. I thought about the conversations I'd had that morning in Nashville about how black and white people are still segregated in neighborhoods, and now again in schools with the end of busing in Tennessee.

Ms. Hooper does not think that what she did has impacted Whitwell. She does not think anything has changed there. I disagree. Whether it feels like things have changed right now, there is a generation of students at Whitwell Middle School who now understand that anything is possible. Who would have believed they could collect one hundred thousand paperclips, let alone twenty-four million?

Whitwell is now home to a generation of students who understand that bigotry and hatred kill people, and that when you kill people, you alter the course of humanity. One student approached Ms. Hooper in tears as they were counting paper clips, saying she believed that perhaps one of the people killed by the Nazis could have devised a cure for the cancer that was right then killing her grandmother. A generation of students now knows about the world in a way that only a teacher with a dream could have imagined. Students from Whitwell have traveled the world sharing the story of the Paper Clips Project.

This investment in our children may lead to a world where we no longer talk about segregation and bigotry—and, if we dare to imagine it, to a world without genocide. It may start with one small town in Tennessee, but who can begin to count the ripple effect as these children enter the world?

So, there I was in Whitwell, as darkness settled in around us and I concluded the interview with Ms. Hooper. She showed me to the exhibit and asked me to lock up after myself as I left.

With no one around, I entered through the gate and slowly approached the ramp leading to the boxcar. I remember saying out loud to myself, "Really, Dafna? A Nazi boxcar, at night, alone . . . in the middle of Tennessee?"

Nazi Boxcar in Whitwell, TN

I stood there in the center of that car and dared not close my eyes. I felt souls all around me and pleaded with myself not to hear them. In many ways, my heart was paralyzed, for here in Tennessee the souls of my ancestors were not forgotten, their deaths were not in vain. The students of Whitwell, championed by Ms. Hooper, will be sure to remember them and will tell their story for many years to come. As they do so, another generation will come and learn that hatred does not build the future. Dedication, community, and respect for others do.

I still face my demons of fear when I see symbols like swastikas or even the Confederate flag, but now I've learned to look deeper for the Ms. Hoopers out there who may, through their work, put an end to the ideology behind those symbols.

I had demons, many of them. I was forced to work through them very consciously every week of the Journey. When it came to facing these demons head on, I figured out that there was a lot in it for me. My mind could think more clearly without them. My heart could connect more freely without them. The stories I shared with you were far less tainted without them.

As you answer "What's in it for me?" for yourself and your community, take that first step and face off with the demons that may try to derail you. Own them. Thank them for their service. Then set them free so you can achieve what you so desire.

Chapter 26
I found prejudice—my own

Prejudice: pre-judging. Judgment of any kind, unchecked, can be a subtle undoing. So subtle you may not even realize it is going on.

Growing up Jewish in Cincinnati provided plenty of opportunities for experiencing antisemitism. Most of it came in the form of ignorant comments, like when a local plumber asked my skullcap-wearing stepfather, "Are you folk Jews?" When my father replied, "Yes, we are Jewish," he asked, "Where's your all's horns and tails?" I was twelve years old, and I was shocked. I had no idea why the Roto-Rooter tech had asked my father that question. Why would he even think we'd have horns and tails?

My father explained how the racist theory stemmed from a painting of Moses descending Mount Sinai and how it spread through the underbelly of antisemitic sentiment. Until the age of eleven, I had lived on the East Coast. I had been surrounded by Jewish communities and people who knew their Jewish neighbors, so these types of ignorant comments had never reached me. I began to learn about hatred and the world that year. I also began to form my own belief systems and values. I promised myself that I would not judge someone by the color of their skin or the name of their Lord. I believed that I had, by my mother's example, learned not to harbor any prejudice.

Qadir Aware brought me to a moment of truth. A moment I did not ever expect to face. In that moment, I had to come to terms with the fact that I *did* harbor prejudices. I did not think I had a prejudiced bone in my body, yet as I prepared for my first interview with a Muslim man, I was nervous. Certainly, there was no rationale for my fear.

Qadir, a short, stocky, brown-skinned Middle Eastern man whose deep wrinkles attested to a life of war, was a former Kurdish freedom fighter. Before becoming an American, Qadir spent his days as a refugee fighting the Iraqis for his family's freedom.

Dafna and Qadir Aware

When he was given an opportunity to seek refuge in the United States, Qadir made the difficult decision to leave his parents and siblings behind and take his young wife to America. Despite being a skilled engineer, Qadir, who spoke no English, found a job cleaning floors in a community center when he and his wife were placed in South Dakota.

Qadir was fairly certain that the people of South Dakota had never come face to face with a Muslim man from the Middle East. He could recount with alacrity the number of times he was spat upon and how many people crossed the street to avoid walking near him. He also recalled, with a bit more humor, how many motor vehicle tickets he received because no one had explained to him the rules of the American road.

With hard work and carefully thought-out plans, Qadir set his family up to achieve the American dream. He was doing OK, but it was not enough for Qadir. He had a unique understanding of the plight of the refugee and the immigrant. He also knew that places not known for great diversity, like South Dakota, were popular destinations to place immigrants. His own experience, echoed by many immigrants who followed his arrival in South Dakota, drove him to seek a solution to an "invisible problem."

Qadir sought a relationship with the governor of South Dakota and implored him to build a center for diversity. Qadir's self-worth blossomed when then-Governor George Speaker Mickelson agreed and promised to work on this. Soon after their meeting, the governor died tragically in a plane crash. It took Qadir a few more years and a lot more effort, but he was not going to let his dream die. He knew how much help he had needed and how much he could provide.

Thirty years after first coming to our country, the Qadir Aware I met was now an American man, bringing immigrants into the communities of South Dakota with a grace that had not been afforded him. Diversity continues to grow in this Middle American city. Everyone, from fifth- and sixth-generation South Dakotans to those just off the tarmac, is benefiting from Qadir's work.

Qadir's dedication to making this transition easier on both the immigrant and the South Dakotan almost seemed unwarranted. Why on earth would he care to improve the lives of the South Dakotan who spat on him when he arrived, and the one who publicly yelled at him and his children "to go back where you came from" after 9/11? A simple man at heart, Qadir truly believes, "If you can just understand a little bit and respect, a little bit, where I come from, and I can do the same for you, we can live in harmony."

Qadir's office is filled with awards, as well as pictures of him from his freedom fighting days. A picture of Qadir with the President of the United States is prominently placed in his office. But right next to his desk hangs the most important pictures of all. In a clean, simple frame are beautiful snapshots of his American grandbabies. Qadir has built the American dream and strengthened it for every person who walks through the doors of the South Dakota Cultural Diversity Center.

Qadir Aware

I left feeling bad about myself. I had been truly scared before my interview. My name is not your everyday American name. It is a common Israeli name, of which I am very proud, and indeed, Qadir started the interview by asking about my name. He, too, was feeling me out. So there we sat, Kurdish Muslim and Israeli Jew, both of us American and proud to be.

Qadir Aware and his family

Both of us were holding on to deep histories of war and unrest in our respective parts of the Middle East. Both of us were trying to make this country, which is our home, stronger. I respectfully gave him my deepest and sincerest thanks for who he is and what he stands for. From what I have been told by friends who have studied the Koran and the Islamic faith, I understand that, at its roots, Islam is a religion of peace. People like Qadir truly live that. And for all our differences, we are simply a cousin away on DNA charts. He is truly a relative. How I wished I could have had such a conversation in Israel.

Recognizing once more the humanness of myself, I resolved not to let fear become involved, whomever I was going to meet. I was going to consciously choose to reserve or remove any judgment before I embarked upon an interview. At the core of this Journey, I was simply looking for people making a real difference in this coun try. How could that be a person who would want to hurt me or who wished me ill? I had to have faith. I had to fully open myself up in a way that I had been able to avoid in the past by keeping myself out of certain situations. This was not my first interaction with a Muslim or an Arab or even a Palestinian. In my life, I have been fortunate to interact with people of many nationalities and faiths, but it always seemed to be on my terms and my turf. I had entered Qadir's turf, and he welcomed me in.

Several months later, when I had the absolute honor of meeting Reza Jalali, a professor at the University of Maine, that fear didn't present itself. Reza was a tall, vibrant man with a regal appearance and an easy smile that highlighted his warm brown eyes. Reza

Dafna and Reza Jalali

was a refugee from the Iranian section of Kurdistan. I was fully excited to meet this man and learn about his work in the state that some call "the whitest state in the nation." Like Qadir, Reza worked to make life easier and more diversity-friendly for the people of many colors who come to Maine through their own searches for asylum and in pursuit of a life free from religious and racial persecution.

Dafna interviewing Reza Jalali

When Reza welcomed me into his home, I felt at home. The warmth, the culture, the hospitality of the Middle East are unprecedented. While learning from Reza, I felt a pang that became so familiar throughout my Journey: I wished that I could be a part of his community. Reza co-teaches a class with a rabbi to show the students how similar Jews and Muslims truly are at their core. He is a person who gives me hope that not only will prejudice decrease here, but perhaps one day, dialogues like those he and the rabbi have will happen around the world.

Perhaps the Rezas out there can give my daughter what she has wished for out loud so many times: a world without hatred and war. She's an old soul, that little girl of mine.

Chapter 27
I found myself as Mom

I know it may seem silly, or even ignorant, but I really did not set out on this Journey to learn about myself. When the journalist who sat on my board said to me one afternoon, "Dafna, this story is going to be about you," I fought him on it. In my mind, this was not supposed to be about me at all. When my first TV news piece aired, the story focused on the person I was meeting, but the comments from viewers attacked me personally. Mostly, the attackers criticized me as a mother. I learned a lot about my children during my Journey.

When I finally got to "do Colorado," my final state visit back at home, the kids joined me as I interviewed the husband-and-wife team my son nominated. My daughter, who was about nine at the time of the interview, did not want to sit and watch and wandered off. My son, then seven years old, promised he'd sit quietly and begged me to let him watch. We were at the SAME Café.

The café was founded by Brad and Libby Burke, a young hipster couple. She was short with brown, wavy hair, and he was tall and skinny, sporting a neatly trimmed reddish beard. Brad was a computer guy, and Libby was an elementary school teacher. The SAME Café was the answer to "How do we create a place where

Dafna and Brad and Libby Burke

people in need can get a wholesome meal in a safe and respectful fashion?" SAME—So All May Eat—was dreamed up on an airplane on the back of a napkin. Brad and Libby, who had volunteered in soup kitchens for years, serving food they themselves would never eat, threw in all the money they had to make their dream a reality. After all, they figured all they had to lose was money. What the community stood to gain was priceless. My son had learned about the dynamic duo on a field trip with his class two years before the Journey. They made such an impact on him before he was six that at seven, he still remembered every detail of their story.

My son, who can be like the Tasmanian Devil—always in motion—sat silently next to me for two hours. At one point, he laid his head on my lap while continuing to listen. At no point did he fidget. Nor did he daydream for even an instant. I had promised him that when I was finished with the interview, he would have an opportunity to ask a question. As I wrapped up, he tapped me on the leg to make sure I had not forgotten the promise. "OK," I told him, "it's your turn. What would you like to ask?" I don't know what I thought he'd ask, but after five hundred interviews, I was certain I had my interviewing skills down pat.

My young son sat tall in his seat, his incredibly inquisitive eyes looking directly at Libby. His question astonished me, both because it showed he had listened intently to the entire conversation, and because it was not a question I had even thought to ask. "Why is it that you only serve organic foods?" he asked. This simple question added an important detail to the story.

For so many years, Brad and Libby had served food in soup kitchens where they themselves would not eat. I had not thought to ask them why not. Brad and Libby believed that organic food has higher quality and nutrient value. They believed in eating local produce from farmers in the

The SAME Café

immediate Denver area. They believed that when you give, you give what you yourself would want to receive and nothing less. This principle is what drives them every day. Had my son not asked that question, a vital part of the story would have been inadvertently glossed over.

Filled with pride at my son's interviewing skills, I went in search of the missing girl with ants in her pants. I found her washing dishes in the café's kitchen, a huge smile on her face and her blue eyes simply glittering. She had been eager to help the guests of the café have a wonderful experience. She found her own way to become a part of the SAME Café family. On the spot, she decided she wanted to have her birthday party there in the coming weeks so she could introduce her friends to the beauty of the SAME Café.

The SAME Café kitchen

My children humble me. Through their eyes I saw the Journey and the people I met anew, without grown-up biases, without tainted life history. Untattered. Innocent.

From Georgia to Texas, through New Mexico, to Arkansas, and on to New York, I saw sunrises and sunsets. I captured landscapes while zooming down the highways. I hugged old friends and met new ones. I learned of struggles and triumphs. I watched people model being accountable and making the world a better place. I wrote blog entries, booked plane tickets, and got parking tickets. I got lost, got found, learned to use a compost toilet, and bought a GPS device. Each week flew by, and whenever I returned home to the role of mommy, my children would pummel me with questions and tell me who they wanted me to interview when I "did" Colorado.

My children are my greatest gifts. They are creative, they are bright, and they are beautiful. No bias here; I'm their mom. My daughter came along five years into my marriage and my son shortly after. They were very wanted and loved from the moment they were conceived. I regularly thank them for giving me the gift of being their parent. I want them to know they are both loved and respected.

Separating from them on a regular basis as part of a post-divorce parenting plan suggested by the state of Colorado was the hardest thing that I, and I'm certain their father, ever had to do. Kids get caught in the upheaval of divorce. Children are innocent to the cause of divorce, yet they bear the weight of the aftermath. Certainly, we parents hope that the divorce will ultimately give them a better life, a life where both Mommy and Daddy are happy. But it is hard for kids. It is also hard for parents to feel that "better life" when they sit crying at the foot of an empty bed, missing their children on the other parent's night.

Each lonely night I sat there, singing to myself the evening prayers I had sung to my children from their very first night outside of my womb. The notes took on a hollow tone as they mixed with the tears flowing down my cheeks.

While planning out the Journey, I felt almost lucky that I was divorced—almost. I never could have done this Journey when I was married. Even before the Journey and divorce, my ex did not like it when I traveled; it was hard on him and hard on the kids. Even divorced, he prefers when I'm in town; it just feels more comfortable "in case anything happens." I planned out my weeks to travel only on the days the kids were with their dad. In my mind, the kids would not miss me, as they would not have been with me anyway.

How wrong I was. Many times throughout the year, my eight-year-old daughter would cry, "Why do you have to go, Mommy? I'm going to miss you." I would ask her what she would like me to do and remind her, "This is your time with Daddy, right?" She would agree that it was her time to be with Daddy. But for all the rationale that I could put behind it, I was not a mile away, and that meant she missed me. I cried when she cried to me on the phone. I ached when I got a call from the babysitter that Gavi had a fever and their dad did not have any Tylenol in the house. I was hundreds of miles away and there was nothing I could do.

I was not shy about telling people that part of what I loved so much about the Journey was not being at home alone without my children. Being in my house at night with only echoes of the sounds of playing and with no little bodies sleeping soundly in their beds was simply excruciating. I avoided that pain by not being at home.

For all the pain of separation, my children showed me how proud they were of me. The moment during the middle of my Journey when my daughter asked me to speak to her class as her "hero" caught me off guard. Tears began flowing from my eyes. "Those are happy tears, Mommy, right?" she asked. And there were the times my son would tell everyone, from the waitress at a restaurant to his school friends, about his mom. He'd say, "Have you heard about the Journey? You should go to 50in52journey.com, that's my mom." These were moments of clarity. My kids totally understood the Journey, and they were proud that I was doing it.

I was taught, perhaps like many of you, that we sacrifice for our children. My mother made many sacrifices for my well-being and for my brothers. When she and I discussed this Journey, she questioned, as did the anonymous commenters on the internet, whether the choices I was making were right for my children. It was less about whether they were right for me.

The first blog post I ever wrote was about the differences, generational perhaps, in the lessons I received from the powerful female influences in my life.

Before my divorce, my grandmother worried that my marriage was failing because I earned more money than my husband. She taught me to talk things out with him but to always defer. She was a master at being the strong matriarch while giving the appearance of power and authority to my grandfather.

My mother was a child of the sixties. She burned her proverbial bra, walked out of class, and sat in the streets for equality in education. Then she married and became the mom who gave up everything for her children. Everything, that is, except being stuck in the wrong marriage.

I take those lessons seriously. I talk with Michael. We make tough decisions together. I fight for equality, standing up for an equal, or better, paystub instead of burning my bra. I don't need one anymore, anyway. (That's a whole nother Oprah . . .)

The lessons I leave for my son and daughter can only be modeled. So what if I had not traveled to all fifty states collecting stories and sharing them with you? Would you have suffered? Unlikely. Some who

Dafna and her grandmother

Dafna and her mother

received grants and donations as a result of my interviews may have failed to continue their work in the same way, but we'll never know.

I do know that I would be different. In that vital moment a hundred or so pages back and many moons ago, Michael held my face in his hands and uttered the words, "This is too important not to do." Had he instead said, "You are right, this is a lottery pipe dream, but I love you anyway," my world would have continued. Perhaps I would have modeled "responsibility" for my children and slipped away from this world quietly, giving in to depression. I stand firmly by the path I chose and was supported in choosing.

When my children reflect on their role models, I hope they learn to find a partner who supports their dreams, to take risks to achieve, to never establish too strong a comfort zone, to love deeply, and to live their dreams. When they were little and dreaming up adventures while riding in the back seat of the car, I always told them, "Nothing is impossible." Genetically sarcastic, they would retort, "Eating Earth is impossible." I'd peek in the rearview mirror at their glib little faces and say, "You can do it, one bite at a time."

Chapter 28
What happened next? I learned that the Journey had just begun

As the wheels touched down at Denver International Airport that third week of December 2009, I began to cry. I had taken my final flight. I was home from my Journey. My head was filled with more questions than answers. My heart was overflowing as I thought of the road ahead. I grabbed my gear and sprinted through the airport to my Michael, who I knew would be waiting for me as I came up the escalators. He stood there, his face reflecting the weariness I felt, with a bouquet of roses in his hands. We stood there in the middle of that great hall, just holding tightly to one another. We were not certain about what lay ahead.

Only a few weeks earlier, CBS Sunday Morning had traveled with my mother and me on my Journey visit to Arizona. They put together an unbelievable nine-minute piece about the Journey. We were in no way prepared for the response we received. As the show aired on the East Coast, a full hour before airing in Denver, people began to tweet me. They quoted me as saying, "It takes a little crazy to make a difference." I couldn't remember saying it, and I was truly perplexed!

Then I began to receive emails at the rate of one per minute for the next twenty-four hours. They were mostly from people thanking me for inspiring them. Some were harsh, and criticized me for reasons I'll never quite fully understand. There were requests from producers to do reality shows. There were requests to meet and collaborate, from local foundations seeking to do similar work. Michael and I were overwhelmed. Our web hosts asked us to find other hosting because our web traffic had not only crashed our site but also affected the rest of the sites they hosted.

When the piece finally aired in Denver, I watched it with my children while hiding my face behind a couch pillow. I was so afraid of what I would see. I should not have worried. The team from CBS was amazing, and they told a beautiful story. And, wouldn't you know it, I did say, "It takes a little crazy to make a difference." Because indeed it does.

We were certain that the opportunities being presented would help us continue to tell the stories we had gathered and capture more. Yet, as we had been so fond of saying throughout the Journey, "Man planned, G-d laughed."

Five months after I finished my travels, I found lumps in each breast. While they were not yet cancerous, we were not going to take any risks. I moved in with Michael so he could take care of me and my kids, and I underwent a bilateral mastectomy. Right after the surgery, the producer we had been working with to create a reality show in the theme of the Journey tragically died of a massive aneurysm. She was just forty-five.

In between surgeries for reconstruction, I continued to develop workshops and keynotes based on all I had seen and learned. I traveled all over the state and the country, speaking and training. The Journey was "elevating, empowering and engaging people in the art of community problem solving." We worked with schools, teachers, nonprofits, and businesses. I spoke to very large groups and very small groups.

Meanwhile, I was tired and sick from the surgeries. Every time I felt a little better, it seemed time for my next surgery. While all these surgeries were going on, my son began to struggle. I became very depressed and stopped writing about the Journey. I had not finished my book about it, and that fact hung over my head like a cloud. Every time I'd speak to a group and invariably get a question from the audience about whether I'd written a book, I'd say, "The book is almost done." Inside, I'd die a little bit more because I felt certain that I was never going to finish it.

I sank even further when Michael and I lost our unborn son. I was five months pregnant and so desperately wanted to have this baby with this man I love so much. Our "Peanut" had a heart defect and died five months into the pregnancy. I didn't know if I could recover. I wasn't sure I wanted to.

A full year after I lost the baby, Michael and I had a silly argument that led to tears. Then I made a statement that showed the true depth of my depression. I looked at Michael, the man who encouraged me, nursed me, fed me, and loved me, and said, "Sometimes I think you don't like me very much." Deflated, Michael looked at me and said, "I just want my wife back." With those words, he once again saved me and brought me back to life. I realized I kind of wanted me back, too.

So, here we are. I'm back, and I'm ready to share this Journey with you. There is a collection of stories I wrote while I traveled and 375 videos on my website www.journeyinstitute.org—read them, watch them, and be inspired to do and be you.

Take the mantle of "crazy" and let it drive you to take the steps necessary to embrace whatever Journey life has in store for you. Know, as these stories show, that no matter what you look like, what you sound like, how old you are, or how much money or education you have, you too can solve a problem in your community. As for me, I'm already itching to take my next Journey. I want to do this all over again, this time on all seven continents.

So now it is your turn! What did you write down when I asked you to pen three things that you complain about in your community? What did you write in the margins of the pages? What stirred inside of you as you read the stories?

Think about the outcomes you seek. Think about the people who will join your team and help you get there. Take strength from all those who have gone before you. I know you can do it. I believe in you.

As for my answer to the young woman who asked me what it feels like to change someone's life, I'm still not so certain I can claim that. I do promise to keep trying every day to help people take control of their own lives and make the changes that will help them and their communities.

I can, however, tell you what it feels like to change my own life, to bring back my power, to embrace my own Journey. That feels amazing.

I now gift that amazing to you.

ABOUT THE AUTHOR

Dafna Michaelson Jenet is the founder and Journeywoman behind the 50in52 Journey in which she travelled to all 50 United States and Washington D.C within the 52 weeks of one year to find, highlight, and elevate "ordinary people doing extraordinary things", solving problems and building community.

She has been interviewed by the late great Maya Angelou on Oprah's Radio Network, been featured by CBS Sunday Morning, and travelled around the world to empower people of all ages into action. She continues her work from lessons learned during her Journey through writing, speaking, and workshops she created to help inspire and engage people to take action in their own communities.

In 2016, Michaelson Jenet was elected to the Colorado House of Representatives where she served seven years before moving to serve in the Colorado State Senate.

JOURNEY INSTITUTE PRESS

Journey Institute Press is a non-profit publishing house created by authors to flip the publishing model for new authors. Created with intention and purpose to provide the highest quality publishing resources available to authors whose stories might otherwise not be told.

JI Press focusses on women, BIPOC, and LGBTQ+ authors without regard to the genre of their work.

As a Publishing House, our goal is to create a supportive, nurturing, and encouraging environment that puts the author above the publisher in the publishing model.

Storytellers Publishing is an Imprint of Journey Institute Press, a division of 50 in 52 Journey, Inc.

Final note. The world of publishing has changed dramatically. This has also affected authors and their ability to let readers know about their books. Today, most people buy books based on word of mouth.

If you would like to help this author, please consider leaving an honest review of this book on retail sites and book community sites such as Goodreads.

www.ingramcontent.com/pod-product-compliance
Lightning Source LLC
Chambersburg PA
CBHW052113030426
42335CB00025B/2965